A PRACTICAL GUIDE TO WORKING IN THEATRE

A PRACTICAL GUIDE TO WORKING IN THEATRE

GILL FOREMAN

Methuen Drama

First edition 2009

Methuen Drama
A & C Black Publishers Ltd
36 Soho Square
London W1D 3QY
www.methuendrama.com

Copyright © 2009 Gill Foreman

Gill Foreman has asserted her right under the Copyright,
Designs and Patents Act, 1988, to be identified as the author
of this work

ISBN 978 0 71368 767 5

A CIP catalogue record for this book is available from the
British Library

This book is produced using paper that is made
from wood grown in managed, sustainable forests.
It is natural, renewable and recyclable. The logging and
manufacturing processes conform to the environmental
regulations of the country of origin.

Typeset by RefineCatch Limited, Bungay, Suffolk

Printed by the MPG Books Group, Bodmin, Cornwall

Contents

This book is dedicated to the memory of my grandmother Eleanor

Introduction

Every evening, in theatres across the world, as the lights begin to dim and the chatter falls away to silence, somewhere in the darkness a quiet voice murmurs into a headset: 'House lights out. Act One beginners, please . . .' For the audience, thus begins two hours or so spent in an alternative reality – the universe of a play, summoned up from wood and fabric made to look like glass and stone, peopled by actors pretending to be someone else, and orchestrated by dozens of unseen helpers whom the audience rarely notice – because when we go to the theatre, how many of us truly understand the range of people and skills that have combined to make our evening's entertainment?

Most of us will encounter the box-office staff who sell us our tickets, ushers, bar staff and programme sellers, but what about everyone else who made our evening possible?

Theatre is a unique combination of crafts. Weeks before a play opens an extraordinarily dedicated group of people work long hours on low salaries to spin magic from ordinary stuff – cheap wine glasses from a local discount store will be painted and painstakingly gilded to resemble the finest medieval Venetian crystal; fabric from a bargain bin will be dyed, starched and treated to become a beautiful and luxurious costume. Lights will be hung, angled and coloured so that you will believe it's a bright midsummer's day in the middle of December and carpenters will create entire worlds of concrete and steel out of plywood and polystyrene. Each department is working towards that opening night, that fixed moment in time when everything combines together in front of a live audience. It's unlike anything else in entertainment, and for those involved produces an energy that can't be replicated in the recorded arts of film and television.

A Guide to Working in Theatre explores and explains the work of each theatrical department. Each chapter attempts to get inside the production process from that department's point of view and includes interviews with those actually doing the work.

Finally, this book is dedicated to all of those creative but invisible stage people – you won't necessarily meet them, but they do what they do because it's their passion and because they want you to have an amazing evening. Live theatre is an exciting, challenging and sometimes difficult medium and it needs enthusiastic, well-trained and skilled practitioners to ensure its future. I hope you will decide to be one of them.

Acknowledgements

This book would not have been possible without the time and generosity of those friends and colleagues in the industry who agreed to be interviewed for this book. I would particularly like to thank those at the Royal Shakespeare Company, the National Theatre and Bristol Old Vic for their advice and insight. I'd also like to thank Peter Wild for his meticulous proofing and advice, and Kate Wolstenholme for reading the manuscript. Thanks to Jackie at Voicescript for transcribing the many hours of interviews so carefully. And finally to my editor Mark Dudgeon at Methuen Drama for putting up with a great deal to see this through.

CHAPTER 1

An introduction to the theatre industry

Drama – the desire to perform or enact a story – is as old as the human race itself: for as long as people have gathered together they have told stories, of themselves, of the things that surround them, and of the issues that preoccupy their community. Rituals and ceremonies have evolved until at some point, rather than tell the story, the community, or members of the community decide to act it out. This pattern can be traced in almost every civilisation that has existed on Earth. However, a communal love of story and play-acting is not the same thing as a professional theatre, where those who take part earn their living.

Professional theatre in England was the invention of Elizabeth I and her government, and its first stars were Christopher Marlowe and William Shakespeare. I suspect, though, that even they would be amazed to see how it has developed!

In this chapter we'll explore the professional theatre landscape and seek to understand the structure of the industry as well as the process of a production.

The professional theatre industry today is extremely diverse and embraces everything from small independent theatre companies to large corporate entertainment conglomerates. There are commercial producers and small, locally funded community arts centres. There are large, national state theatre companies, regional venues and international companies, as well as tiny one-person outfits making street performance. They are all wildly different – so how are we to make sense of it all?

The two industry sectors

Professional theatre can be roughly divided in two sectors, the commercial and the subsidised. Modern subsidised theatre is chiefly funded by central and local government, while commercial theatre receives no state or grant funding, operating in the same way as any commercial business, its money coming from the profits of previous productions and funds from investors.

Commercial theatre

At the heart of any commercial theatre company will be a producer or team of producers. They will have established a knack for finding 'hit' shows and they will have a loyal group of financial backers or investors, known in the industry as 'angels'. These angels will invest money in a production for a percentage of the show's profits, once it has paid for its costs. The commercial sector is unlikely to stage the work of a new or unknown playwright, or cast unknown actors in lead parts. Instead, lead roles will be played by well-known actors, often from film or television.

Commercial theatre companies rarely own their own venues – they lease a theatre from one of the commercial theatre landlords for a fixed term, usually between six weeks and three months initially, with an option to extend the term if the show is a success. Some of the West End's most successful productions have been running for decades – the longest-running production being Agatha Christie's *The Mousetrap*, which opened at the New Ambassadors Theatre in 1952 and is still running today, in its fifty-seventh year, at the St Martin's Theatre.

Subsidised theatre

A subsidised theatre is one that makes no profit, and operates using funds donated by a patron. In the UK, subsidised theatre involves a whole sector of companies and their chief patron is the British government. The Treasury, via the Arts Council, distributes a series of grants that fund arts organisations, including theatre companies, in one of two ways. A key list of theatres receive annual *capital* grants to fund their day-to-day operations as well as the productions that they stage. In addition, the Arts Council also issues *project* grants, ranging from a few hundred pounds to multiple thousands of pounds, to theatre companies in order that they stage a specific production or project. There are also regional Arts Councils that do the same for regional theatre companies. Some companies also receive funding from their local county, district or town councils.

Subsidised theatre companies must spend government money properly and report regularly on how they do so. They cannot make a profit and they must keep ticket costs at a level that make them accessible to all. In addition to this, the conditions of the grant given include being a resource for their local community as well as carrying out education and participation programmes.

Types of theatre organisation

Within the broad division of the commercial and subsidised sectors there are further subdivisions as to the type and structure of the organisation. These structures are not exclusive to one or other sector, but exist in both.

Receiving houses

Receiving houses are theatres that produce no original work of their own. Instead, they host or 'tour in' other people's productions, usually those of commercial production companies. Much of London's West End is made up of commercial receiving houses. Many of these are owned by entertainment conglomerates and, more recently, commercial producers who see the value of owning theatres in which they can stage their work, rather than paying rent to a theatre landlord. A receiving theatre is run by a very small management team who will hire in additional staff to suit the production coming in.

Outside the West End, runs are short, sometimes just a week, and often for part of a tour prior to or after the production has played in the West End.

Producing house

Also referred to as a building-based theatre company, most but not all of these companies are subsidised theatre companies who make and stage their own original productions. They have a significant number of permanent staff, from administrators and office-based departments, to the full range of production departments such as scenic construction, wardrobe, lighting and sound.

Producing houses often enter into co-production deals with two or three other building-based theatre companies, particularly when staging a more expensive or risky play. In this arrangement, the companies share the costs and the profits of the production, which will open at one venue and then move on to the other theatres involved in the deal.

Subsidised, building-based producing houses usually have an artistic policy from which their programme extends, and must ensure that ticket costs are reasonably affordable to all. These sorts of theatre companies include our state theatre companies, the Royal Shakespeare Company and the National Theatre, as well as many of the country's regional repertory theatres.

Independent production companies

Most independent production companies are commercial operations of the kind discussed earlier. They are usually headed up by one or more successful producers who may have three or four shows in production at any one time, and because production companies need small overheads they have a limited number of permanent staff.

While the producer will choose the play to be staged and have some involvement in the casting, every other aspect of the production will be contracted out to separate organisations, from the marketing and PR to the building of the set. Production companies are rarely based in a theatre building; they are more often installed in suites of offices close to a town or city's theatre district.

A new production will be rehearsed in rented rehearsal rooms and transfer to the theatre just a week or so prior to opening. The theatre will be hired, initially on a short lease, so that should the production fail, a producer can close the show without incurring too many losses. If the production is a success the rental contract will be renegotiated and the lease extended.

Independent theatre companies

Not all subsidised theatre companies are based inside theatre buildings, and for many small to medium theatre companies receiving only project funding, owning and running a theatre building would be impossible. Instead, these companies are usually based in commercial business properties, maybe warehouses or converted factory premises, sometimes church halls or disused schools – places that offer the company some sort of rehearsal space and a number of offices. Sometimes an independent theatre company, like an independent production company, will be office-based, hiring its rehearsal spaces as and when required.

The independent theatre company, while not based inside a traditional theatre building, may have significant links with their local building-based theatre, regularly staging their work at the venue or developing projects together. Independent theatre companies regularly embark on tours of venues within their region or across the country.

One of the key aspects of such a company is that they are often driven by a specific set of ideas or a particular performance philosophy. They will have a permanent team of company members – not as large as a building-based theatre company, but larger than a production company.

Fringe theatre and fringe festivals

In 1947, during the annual International Edinburgh Festival, a group of small theatre companies rented space around the fringes of the official festival in order to present a series of plays. None of these companies was part of the festival, but by roaming the streets close to the official venues, handing out leaflets and publicising their shows, they drew an audience and thus the Edinburgh Fringe Festival, the UK's first 'fringe' festival, was born. This style of theatre, named for the fact that it lay both physically and artistically on the edge of traditional and established theatre, was then coined for a whole genre. In the 1960s it became an umbrella term used to embrace a wide range of new and experimental theatre styles. It tended to imply performers who were engaged in seeking out new methods of staging as well as new philosophies for creating work, and because many of these groups could not access commercial or mainstream venues, they sought to convert alternative spaces, such as industrial buildings, open-air venues, decommissioned churches and church halls, and in particular the old function rooms in large public houses that had mostly fallen out of use.

This new theatre was more intimate, more edgy than the plush world of velvet-covered seats and wood veneer, and attracted a whole new audience of young and adventurous theatregoers. The very nature of this type of work is transitory and changeable. Some of the fringe companies that were created in the 1960s are today part of the theatre establishment, while many have disappeared, only to be replaced with a new wave of young theatre-makers seeking to invent and innovate.

Fringe theatre is the seedbed of new theatre, but it is largely unfunded and unprofitable. At one time it was possible for new, young companies to apply for and get project funding from the Arts Council, but this has been increasingly difficult since the 1980s. Today, companies produce work with little or no money and actors and crew often work for free or on profit-share agreements. For those in the early stages of their careers, fringe theatre can offer opportunities to experiment with and develop their craft, and in the last three decades, it has repeatedly been the source of leading new playwrights, actors and designers.

Systems of production

Each theatre company has its own approach to programming its plays and productions, but will traditionally follow one of three approaches: repertory, repertoire or stagione. The latter was once the preserve of opera companies, but is becoming increasingly popular due to rising costs and the influence of Central European approaches to theatre production.

Repertory system

The current repertory system, an adaptation of a much older style of production process, consists of a season of between six and eight plays. Each play is separately cast and rehearses for three weeks before opening. Once open, it will run for a further three weeks while the next production moves into the rehearsal room. Generally, there will be a different cast and crew for each production. Some building-based companies have more than one theatre, usually a smaller studio space where they might present more experimental work, which may also rehearse for longer.

Repertoire system
This is a complex system requiring considerable resources in terms of planning and technical ability. In the repertoire system, the plays for a season are decided in a similar way to those of the repertory system; however, instead of each show being cast individually, in the repertoire system, a company of actors are cast who will appear in all of the plays, taking a variety of lead and supporting roles. As in the repertory system, rehearsals usually last three weeks, but as one show opens and the next goes into rehearsal, the actors will find themselves rehearsing one play during the day and performing another in the evening.

Unlike the repertory system, where a play runs for three weeks and then finishes, in the repertoire system a play may run for as few as four performances before it is taken off and another put on in its place. However, the initial production is not over. Its set, costumes, props, etc., are stored, and it will be back onstage at regular intervals throughout the season.

Because the plays come in and out of the theatre at regular intervals, they must be stored nearby, and a reasonably sized stage crew be kept on hand to carry out the changeovers. Such changeovers often occur overnight, or in the space of a morning, so the various departments must be able to swap one show for another smoothly and speedily. As for the actors, well, they must remember the lines of several shows at a time. In the largest building-based theatre companies, such as the Royal Shakespeare Company and the National Theatre who have more than one stage, this workload is substantial and requires a staff of several hundred to carry it out.

Stagione system
Until very recently, this approach to programming productions was primarily used by opera and ballet companies, but in Russia and Central Europe, the idea of developing a 'signature' staging of a play that is revived again and again, and plays among a number of other productions, is a familiar one. As more and more of our young directors train and work internationally, these ideas are beginning to influence British theatre programming.

The structure of a producing theatre company

Producing theatre companies are complex organisations but on the whole they are all structured along the same principles. There is an artistic director, an experienced theatre director of some repute, who runs the building and sets the artistic programme alongside the chief executive or executive producer, who is primarily responsible for the financial organisation of the theatre. This pair are supported by their senior management team who are the heads of the theatre's other divisions. The leadership and senior management are regulated by the theatre's board of governors, which is made up of experienced business people who bring valuable commercial skills and advice to the theatre. They also serve as a check, ensuring that money is spent wisely and decisions have been made carefully. The board will often include representatives from the theatre's funding organisations.

A producing theatre will also have a range of staff who work in the technical departments responsible for making and running the shows. In addition, there are creative teams, usually temporary members of the company brought together for one show or season.

Production process

As already discussed, there are a number of approaches to producing plays within a theatre, and different theatres will devote a different amount of time to each stage. In general, there are three parts to the production process. First, pre-production, which is when most of the planning and preparation is done. This period can last anything from six months to a week, depending on the role an individual has within a production – a director will spend a long time preparing a production, while an assistant stage manager might be hired the week before the show goes into production. Next, the production period itself, which lasts between three and six weeks – sometimes longer – and is the most intense period of the cycle. Rehearsals start, the set is built, costumes made and tickets sold. The final production phase is known as 'the run', the period during which the production opens to the audience, plays for a number of weeks and then closes.

Finding out more

Billington, Michael, consultant ed., *Performing Arts: An Illustrated Guide*, Macdonald Educational, 1980
Brockett, Oscar G., and Hildy, Franklin J., *History of the Theatre*, 10th edn, Allyn & Bacon, 2008

Cassell Companion to Theatre, revised edn, Cassell, 1997

Griffiths, Trevor R., *The Theatre Guide*, 3rd edn, A & C Black, 2003

Kennedy, Dennis, ed., *The Oxford Encyclopedia of Theatre & Performance*, Oxford University Press, 2003

Stanton, Sarah, and Banham, Martin, *Cambridge Paperback Guide to the Theatre*, Cambridge University Press, 1996

Zarrilli, Phillip B., et al., *Theatre Histories: An Introduction*, Routledge, 2006

Arts Council of Great Britain – www.artscouncil.org.uk

PeoplePlayUK – www.peopleplayuk.org

Theatrical Management Association – www.tmauk.org

CHAPTER 2

The playwright

Some of the earliest recorded words that survive today are the plays of ancient Athens gentlemen playwrights, living over two thousand years ago. For the modern playwright this can be a daunting inheritance to live up to. However, live theatre is a magical art form that has an immediacy that cannot be matched by the recorded media of television or cinema, and this makes writing for the stage a unique, challenging and hugely rewarding skill. Even those who aspire to write for film and television would do well to begin with writing plays, as most leading screenwriting authorities point to the play as the parent of the screenplay.

So, a daunting ancestry, but the aim of Aeschylus is the same as that of today's playwright: to create a group of characters and a story that, for the audience, reflects some part of their lives back to them in a way they can empathise with and respond to. Great plays observe and comment on human behaviour and have compassion for the human condition. The audience can recognise and engage with the characters involved and follow or share the journey they go through during the action of the play.

Jobs in playwriting

Playwright

The job of a playwright is an odd one. Playwrights spend their days mostly alone trying to invent dialogue for imaginary people, in imaginary situations and imaginary locations. Playwrights must be acute observers of human nature and behaviour, with the ability to translate these observations into their characters. While creativity and imagination seem obvious requirements, a playwright must also have strong research and structural skills to plan and orchestrate the story she or he wants to tell. Playwriting in itself is a poorly paid profession and only the most successful will earn a living from this work. Many write in other forms – for TV or film – or have jobs as lecturers, while some are also novelists or journalists. It is rare to make one's living solely from playwriting.

Literary manager

A literary manager works for a theatre company that regularly stages new plays and adaptations, and a major part of their role is to find and develop new playwrights, as well as liaising with the established playwrights and authors the theatre might commission. The literary manager for a large theatre company will also run a department and employ several staff who carry out a much broader brief of work, from research on specific plays that are being considered for a season, to finding 'lost' plays, as well as seeking out new playwrights. In addition, they will log, read and write reports on all the unsolicited plays that the theatre company are sent and see work by playwrights they are interested in on a regular basis. The literary manager is often tasked with keeping abreast of what's happening in theatre in other countries, looking out for new writers not just at home, but anywhere in the world. It's the literary department that also issues the playwrights' contracts, once they've been commissioned, and liaises with them while they're working for the theatre, ensuring they meet their deadlines and that their royalties are paid.

Dramaturge

The role of the dramaturge in recent times has largely emerged from the United States, although the term is a German one. The role is in parts similar to that of the literary manager, the distinction being that a dramaturge is often more directly engaged in developing the work of an individual writer, acting as a sort of mentor for the playwright both within the rehearsal room and outside it. The dramaturge will also be involved in adapting material from other forms, for example a novel, into the play format, and in the development of play translations. A dramaturge is often a freelance and as such is less involved in the administrative elements of literary management.

Script reader

Script readers are mostly self-employed, and might work for a number of theatres on a freelance basis. Their job is to read plays passed to them by the literary department and prepare a report on a play's quality, its suitability for production and the ability of the writer. Many script readers are young directors, because they have the ability to evaluate a play's potential for productions. The skill of the script reader is to be objective and judge each play on its own merits.

Literary agent

A literary agent represents a playwright's interests, ensuring they are paid adequately for their work, sees that royalties are collected on plays that their clients have already written and looks out for suitable theatres to suggest their clients' work to. There have been truly skilled literary agents who have shaped whole eras of theatrical writing because of the playwrights they have discovered, supported and promoted. Good literary agents do more than just sell plays to theatres; they endeavour to guide new playwrights and find the right sort of commission from the right sort of theatre company at the right time in their career – one that will suit the playwright's style and skills while at the same time offering them positive challenges that enable them to develop their craft.

Production process

Pre-production
Having the idea
So, where does a play come from and how do you start? The idea for a play can come from an overheard conversation, from watching people while sat in a coffee shop, bar or restaurant, from an incident observed, a story in a newspaper, or simply a question the playwright is seeking an answer to. The idea may arrive quickly and fully formed, or may emerge slowly over several days, weeks or months. Whatever the process, the early stages of a play will be about thinking, making notes and asking questions about the story and its characters, rather than writing scenes or dialogue.

A getting started exercise

- While sitting in a public place, look for two people talking. Choose those furthest away so that you can't hear what they are actually saying to each other. Give each of them a name.
- Watch their body language. Who are they? What do they do? How are they related to one another? What sort of conversation are they having?
- Watch two or three exchanges of their conversation and then write down what you think was said. Remember, it must fit with who you think they are, and what their relationship is.

Planning and research
The notion that a playwright has an idea for a play and sits down and starts writing it is unfortunately an unrealistic one. Good plays are the result of much planning and research. Indeed, 90 per cent of the process is about planning.

Some plays will involve complex research in libraries or specialist collections, or require the playwright to make trips to key places that will feature or inform the plot. Unless the playwright writes only about the things she or he knows well – and this would limit their range considerably – this is an essential part of the playmaking process.

To be truly effective, the world of the play must be believable for the audience. If not, it's unlikely that the play will succeed, because if they sense a lack of authenticity in a play's plot or characters, if the facts lack credibility, then the audience will suspect the rest of the play does too.

At the end of the research and planning period, an idea of the play's subject and content will begin to emerge, which the playwright then needs to order it into an outline.

The outline

An outline, sometimes referred to as a synopsis or, to borrow a film term, a treatment, is a scene-by-scene description of what happens and which characters are involved. This outline is backed up by the various strands of research the playwright has conducted, together with character profiles and a backstory to the different events and issues contained within the play. The playwright uses this outline as a guide while making the first draft of the script itself.

Constructing the play

The basic structural elements of a play can be expressed as: exposition and story, character, time and location, or, put in simpler terms, the playwright needs to establish the who? what? why? where? when? and how? of the story that they want to tell. As a playwright develops their ideas, some sense of the structure they want to use will also begin to emerge – the choice of structure being inextricably tied up in what the playwright is trying to communicate.

There are an ever burgeoning number of methods to approach structuring a play, as more and more playwrights and writing gurus publish manuals on how to write plays, and it would be impossible to cover them all here. There are many who think that these approaches are, anyway, simply variations on the original methodology described by Aristotle in the third century BCE.

Exposition and story

Once a playwright establishes the structure of the play, they will explore the way in which the story itself will be revealed, or exposed – hence the term exposition. The plot of a play is how the events in a story are revealed to the audience. For example, in David Hare's *Plenty*, the first scene begins with a naked man asleep on the floor, and a woman seated silently on a packing case. Clearly this is not the beginning of the story, and the events within the play will seek to explain how this moment was reached.

Exposition is a powerful tool when wielded well. Exposition can also work differently for the audience and the characters onstage. Do we the audience find out that Juliet is a Capulet before or after Romeo falls in love with her? We find out before, and what's more we also know she is to be married to someone else. Neither Romeo nor Juliet knows the parentage of the other before they fall in love, and this not knowing increases the consequences of the situation for each of them, while the dynamic of the audience knowing something that the characters do not increases their investment in the story – a device often referred to as dramatic irony – and heightens the sense of tension for audience and characters alike.

Character

Characters are the backbone of the play, because it is through the interactions of the characters that the play's events happen. A play with a solid structure and fantastic plot will not work if the characterisation is poor or inconsistent. Most playwrights have a vague sense of the people involved in their story when they first have their idea, but in order to have them fully inhabit the world of the play, they will take these initial vague notions and develop them into detailed character studies and biographies. Unlike the novelist, a playwright can't give a detailed prose description of their character and their interior and exterior appearance to the audience. Instead, character is revealed bit by bit through what characters do, what they say and what others say about them.

A playwright seeks to develop a series of ideas and characters across the length of a play. A character does not usually walk onstage and introduce themself, or give you their background history as part of an introductory monologue. It is the playwright's skill that reveals these things to the audience. At the beginning of *Romeo and Juliet*, we learn almost everything about Romeo from other people, as they wait for him to arrive, or seek to find his whereabouts. In this brief series of conversations we learn that Romeo falls in love easily, falls in love frequently and is also impatient and quick to anger. All these aspects of his character will have an impact on events. It is only the clumsy dramatist who would have Romeo enter and say: 'Oh dear, I'm really cross because I've fallen in love again!'

Time

Time in theatre works on three levels. The first and most obvious to the audience is real time – the time the play starts and finishes on the evening or afternoon on which they go to see it. This is an important consideration for a playwright. By paying for a ticket and sitting down in their seat, the audience are making a contract with the playwright. They are giving away some of their time in exchange for embarking on the journey of the play. The writer's job is not to waste that time.

Within the world of the play, of course, there are other timelines in operation. Is the play set in the present day, or in a different century? – and, more importantly, how does the writer convey this to their audience? Furthermore, what time span does the dramatic action cover? The events of a day? – a week? – a decade? Other elements – the plot, the theme, etc. – will often determine these factors, but a playwright must consider them before setting out to write the dialogue. Some playwrights favour 'real time' plays, that is stories whose events take place in the real time that the audience is in the theatre, so around two hours.

Ultimately, a play can be set at any time, in the present day or five hundred years ago, but the playwright must decide on it and work out how they will establish this fact for the audience.

Location

Sometimes it will be the location that inspires the play. *Romeo and Juliet* opens with the words: 'Two households, both alike in dignity, in fair Verona, where we lay our scene . . .' This choice was not a random one. In the sixteenth century, the independent northern town of Italy was known for its feuding and vendettas, while Italy was also home to the masquerade – a party where those attending wore masks to hide their identity. Two factors that become important in the events of the play.

Unless it's a deliberate feature of the play's style, shifting location too many times will confuse and disorientate the audience and make the play hard to follow. It will also require several changes of scenery, which slows down the action of the play and makes it expensive to produce. Unless you're writing for a theatre company with a sophisticated backstage operation that involves the ability to shift sets swiftly, usually with the aid of computer technology, then the play will require a large team of stagehands – another critical expense. If the play is being written as part of a commission, then the location will be determined by budgets and scale. A play that is designed to tour cannot usually be located in several places requiring several different sets as this would make touring too expensive and time-consuming. That's not to say that the playwright should limit themself; instead, if they need the play to exist in many different locations they must be theatrically creative in how those locations are realised.

Dramatic action

All plays, as part of their plot, require dramatic action, which should not be confused with simple physical action. Dramatic action is more about the internal journey of the characters and the play – from where we start to where we end. Romeo begins as a fairly feckless boy in and out of love and ends as a man prepared to break laws and die for the woman he loves and has married.

In order for an audience to stay in their seats they need to have a reason to do so; they need to have some sort of investment in the journey that the characters are going on, and in a play this can be done in several ways, the chief of which is by creating dramatic tension. To create it, the playwright must keep their audience in suspense, keep them wanting more, give them key pieces of information that the characters in the play don't know, but should they find out will have dramatic consequences.

First draft

With the idea developed, the research complete, and outline and a structure decided upon, it is only at this point that the play itself is written. There are today a multitude of books and manuals that aim to teach writers how to write, some incredibly influential, others workaday. But while courses and 'how to' books might be useful in the early stages, most successful playwrights would say that they ultimately stifle creativity and original thought by making the new writer feel that there is a formula for writing a good play. There are guidelines certainly, but new writers often enter the profession trying to break the rules, not stick to them. These then are some of the things a playwright considers when writing the first draft.

Theme

It is usually in the opening moments of the play that the writer introduces another key element of the piece – the controlling idea or theme of the play, often by the choice of words and ideas that reoccur. If we examine the first eighty lines of Shakespeare's *Romeo and Juliet*, where two of the Capulet servants are talking, the words that consistently reoccur are 'Montague', 'dog', 'strike', 'sword', 'weapon', 'moved', 'run' and 'fear' – all words that express one of the key themes of the whole play. Conversely, the last hundred lines of the same scene, which involve Romeo and his cousin Benvolio, continually focus on the word 'love'.

Editing the first draft

Once the first draft is complete most playwrights prefer to take a break from the script before reading or thinking about what they've written, in order to gain some distance and perspective on the creative investment of writing the play. This pause may be numbered in days, weeks or months, but there will come an inevitable point at which the first draft must be read and edited.

Editing is the act of reading back over what has been written and making notes, and notes might be as mundane as a reminder to check a fact or name of a character referred to or not seen. Notes might be about typos made while typing the script, or the format used. However, the most significant purpose of the editing process is to work out, by reading and imagining the play, what works and what doesn't. The editing process might point up the need for changes to entire characters or sequences of the play and is a useful part of detaching from the play as a creative work of art and beginning to see it as a technical manual for actors, directors, etc., in how to tell the playwright's chosen story.

For some writers, particularly those at the start of their careers, this is when the support of a mentor or dramaturge can be most useful. They are outside the writing process and can give the playwright objective feedback.

Towards the final draft – the redrafting process

The redrafting of a play is often the most arduous part of the process. Having completed the mammoth task of writing 120 pages of dialogue, many playwrights are reluctant to change anything, but it is wise and usually necessary, to ensure that the play's structure works and is tight enough, the characterisations realistic and consistent, and the action clear and fulfilling. An experienced playwright may make only one revised draft, whereas a new playwright may need to make several; however, if the play is a commissioned one, then the writer will have a strict deadline as to when this process has to end and the script must be ready for rehearsals. It is not designed to be the final version of the play and is usually known as the rehearsal draft.

Types of script

There are two basic sorts of script – the commissioned and the speculative or spec script. When a theatre company wants a particular playwright to write a play exclusively for them, they *commission* it by sending a formal contract to the writer. The commission sets out what the playwright and the theatre company have agreed, the dates for completion of first and subsequent drafts and the fee the writer will be paid. It is rare for an unknown playwright to receive such a commission. Instead, new playwrights will write a speculative script about an issue or subject that interests them and in which they seek to demonstrate their abilities as a writer. They do so without a commission and then send it to theatres in the hope of provoking interest in their work.

Rehearsed reading or workshop

Often with new work, there is an interim stage before the play goes into production, usually in the form of a workshop or a rehearsed reading. In this situation the director, probably the one who will direct the full production, assembles a group of actors and for two or three days they will work on the script in the rehearsal room, with the writer present, trying out the scenes, finding out if everything works. At the end of this period, the play will be presented to an audience of some sort, and given a reading. Actors, script in hand, will give a semi-staged performance. Seated on chairs they will make limited movements, but there will be no set or costumes and only basic lighting. In this way the playwrights can see their play in three dimensions, and find out what works and what needs revising. Some small fringe theatres, which don't have the finances to stage full productions of new work, offer rehearsed readings to playwrights whose work they have read and liked. They will invite a range of people to see this work, and literary agents and literary managers regularly attend rehearsed readings on the lookout for new and interesting writers.

Rehearsal draft

The completion of a first draft is usually the first deadline written into a playwright's contract or agreement. It is not designed to be the final version of the play and is read only by a few individuals within the company that commissioned the work, usually the literary manager, the artistic director and, if appointed, the person who will direct the show. Feedback on the draft will be presented to the playwright and this may range from questions about characters, plots and events, to thoughts on locations or plot structure and can include criticism or direct requests for alterations and changes.

First rehearsal

For the playwright, the moment on the first day of rehearsal, the moment when the cast and crew sit down to read through the play together, can be a nerve-racking one, especially as, in principle, at this point the playwright's work is done. For many playwrights the read-through is their final direct contact with their play, the point at which they must let it go and hand it over to the director, actors and creative team.

Read-through

For a read-through, the whole company will sit down in a rehearsal room in a circle or around a large table and read through the play from beginning to end. With a new play, the writer will start this process by talking about the play, what inspired it and what the play seeks to convey or achieve. The active work of rehearsal will then begin.

Early rehearsal period

Some playwrights are always present in rehearsal, some attend occasionally and some do not like to attend at all, feeling that their job was to write the play, and that having done so, the work is now the responsibility of the director. Some directors prefer the writer to be present, while others forbid it.

In reality, most playwrights would say that their presence is only useful in the early rehearsal period where the play is still being 'fixed'. During this period they can answer actors' questions and offer rewrites of sections that need it. However, once actors begin to learn their lines and establish scenes, constant revision or rewriting becomes distracting or destructive, however tempting it may seem.

Technical week
Marketing and PR

As the production schedule moves into technical week, the focus of the playwright often becomes marketing and PR, working with the relevant departments to promote the play. This might involve giving interviews to local or national media about the play and its production. The entertainment sector is increasingly competitive with a great deal of choice on offer to audiences, so the marketing department must work hard to gain attention. Many playwrights now have their own websites and social networking pages where they will also promote their work.

Publication

Often, the work of the playwright has a second life as a published playtext. Some theatres now include the script in the programme when they produce new work, via special deals with publishers. In this context, the playwright will work with the literary department or manager and an editor from the publisher to keep the manuscript up to date during the rehearsal process, and the initial publication of the script will correspond with the opening of the play.

Opening night

The playwright, where possible, will attend the opening night along with the other creative-team members to support the director and the cast. Their duties on this occasion consist mostly of talking to any journalists or broadcasters present, networking and greeting key invited VIPs. Not all writers are comfortable or at ease in these situations, but producing new plays is costly and involves considerable risk, and most playwrights recognise the need to attend these events in order to support the cause of new writing in theatres. After press night the writer's work is over. The production will continue for the agreed period – usually three to four weeks for a building-based production, or as much as nine to twelve weeks where the production is to tour. In some cases, where a new play is very successful, it could be sold on to a commercial producer who may install it in a theatre on a long-term basis, or put it out on a national or international tour. In these circumstances, the writer may become involved again, making further revisions and participating in promotional activities, but all these circumstances should be covered by the original commission contract or any subsequent adjustments.

Once the production is over, however, the play lives on. It can be revived again and again, and anyone wishing to stage it must pay a fee to do so, and a small percentage of the production's profits as royalties to the author. So despite the effort and personal investment required to write a play, it rewards, both in terms of the effect the playwright may make on his or her audience, and the legacy of a play that can be forever restaged.

Copyright
Copyright is the formal ownership of a work by an author, and a playwright automatically owns the rights to anything she or he writes, unless they assign or sell those rights to someone else. Playwrights should always assert their copyright when sending work to agents, literary managers or potential buyers and a writer does this two ways. The first is to insert the copyright symbol © into the footer of the document in a word-processing tool, followed by the date and the author's name. The second is by adding the formal assertion of copyright to the title page of the document.

The Writers' Guild of Great Britain
The WGGB is a trade union which represents writers for TV, radio, theatre, the fiction and non-fiction book market, poetry, film and the new gaming market, and the organisation negotiates standard working practice agreements and rates of pay with the various commercial bodies that their clients work for.

Things to do

- Read a wide selection of plays from different periods of history. Try to read as many different playwrights as you can.
- Get involved in drama at school and find out how theatre is made.
- Try writing short scenes and then ask your friends to read them back to you – what works and what doesn't?
- Join a young writers' group where possible.

Finding out more

Ayckbourn, Alan, *The Crafty Art of Playmaking*, Palgrave Macmillian, 2003

Daniel, John, *Dramaturgy: A User's Guide*, Central School of Speech & Drama, 1999

Davis, Rib, *Writing Dialogue for Scripts: Effective Dialogue for Film, TV, Radio and Stage*, 3rd revised edn, A & C Black, 2008

Dromgoole, Dominic, *The Full Room: An A–Z of Contemporary Playwriting*, Methuen, 2000

Gooch, Steve, *Writing a Play*, A & C Black, 2004

Grieg, Noel, *Playwriting – A Practical Guide*, Routledge, 2005

Mosse, Kate, *Writers' & Artists' Yearbook*, A & C Black, 2008

Spencer, Stuart, *The Playwright's Guidebook*, Faber and Faber, 2003

Taylor, Val, *Stage Writing: A Practical Guide*, Crowood Press, 2002

Wu, Duncan, *Making Plays: Interviews with Contemporary British Dramatists and Their Directors*, Macmillan, 2000

Getting started

David Edgar

When my mother saw me playing Miss Prism at the age of thirteen at my all boys' school she said, 'Well, it's not going to be acting, is it, dear?' I tried a bit of acting at school, and designing and directing, and, I think, went to university to read drama at Manchester with the idea of becoming a director. But then got caught in the student revolt and became a student journalist and ran the student newspaper and was finding that writing was what I wanted to do. And then I became a journalist for three years, always with the idea that I would write in the evening and, unlike most other people, I managed to do that.

I was peculiarly lucky that Bradford University didn't have a drama department but they had a fellow in theatre who was a young director called Chris Parr [who went on to run the Traverse in Edinburgh and to be a producer at the BBC]. And he noticed that there were a lot of young playwrights emerging and thought, rather than do endless cycles of student productions of the usual suspects, that he would commission small, short plays from aspiring playwrights like Howard Brenton and myself.

I wrote plays as a child for me to act in and I wrote a play at university but, really, the plays that I started writing seriously, and many plays that have gone on, were plays that I wrote for Chris Parr.

I think that I knew quite a lot about the theatre – the theatre was my love as a child and I'd been to it a lot, therefore I didn't have certain problems that later generations of playwrights had. I mean, lots of playwrights of my generation didn't actually go to the theatre much.

I'm not sure I'm patient enough to be a director. I have great admiration for directors. I mean, the amount of repetition involved in both acting and directing, I think would drive me up the wall.

But certainly, I'm not one of those writers who has a desire to direct my own work or to turn into a director. So I think it's partly inclination as well as a particular decision. I mean, the other thing was, I did find that I did get caught up in the student movement at university and, therefore, I had something I wanted to say. Of the crafts, writing is obviously the one that allows you to say things most directly.

What inspires me? . . . Well, I quite like what Stoppard said, and you can see it in his work and you can certainly see it in *Rock 'n' Roll*, it's when two or three different ideas come together, you get something.

I think one of the great functions of the subsidised theatre is to help people round the corners of their careers, that at crucial moments when things are not always going fantastically well, they're helped round the corner by an institutional connection of some sort.

I collect newspaper cuttings. It's the bane of the people I live with.

I do a pretty complete structure and notes on characters and all of that before I start. I now very seldom find that the first draft doesn't take between six and eight weeks and I would increasingly expect to do probably a couple more drafts.

I think there has been a change for the worse and a change for the better. The change for the worse has been a decline in small theatres prepared to do little plays – little in the source terms – which is where my earlier work went on. But there's been a huge increase in forms of writer training. The Birmingham Rep's Transmissions is, I think, an object lesson.

I think peers, whether that peer is teaching a university course or running a weekend or running something like Transmissions, I think peers are really good for the theatre because it is a craft. It does have all kinds of limitations that novels, in particular, and poetry don't.

Undoubtedly, the main advantage of theatre is that it is so cheap and the risks are so low, comparatively, that you can get stuck in. And you can also have much more of a hand in how it goes on and you can change it. You can change it in response. It's much easier. It's more flexible.

I think it's a great advantage, in Britain, that playwrights are unionised and there are agreements which cover big national institutions and the reps and the fringe. That means payment for writers – which should then become a benchmark elsewhere.

And the gains of that, when we first negotiated it thirty years ago, which we have preserved and improved, are firstly the establishment of commission fees so that you get paid while you're writing, as opposed to just writing on spec and then getting a royalty. Secondly, a limit on the participation that theatres have. So, if you've got a big hit down at Theatre Royal, you'll make money out of that success. But if you have a minor success and get it on the radio and get a couple of rep productions, you won't be paying 40 per cent of your income to the original producing theatre, which is a great gain.

And then, thirdly, there's what I've always called the Bill of Rights, which includes the rights to text and integrity – so, a script can't be changed without your permission – but also, crucially, the right to attend rehearsals and be paid for so doing. The payment's really important because it's acknowledging that you have a job in rehearsals and you're protecting your baby, that you have a consultative role in the operation, acting, directing, design. No other country in the world does that. Some countries have the right to attend rehearsals, but nobody has rehearsal payment rights. That's really important.

Stephen Jeffries

I think it was very deep in my psyche that I wanted to write and I certainly wanted to write when I was at school. I remember one half-term going to Woolworths – I was about thirteen – to buy a notebook and starting to write a novel.

I started writing plays when I was about seventeen, eighteen, and then I realised I didn't know anything practically about theatre.

I've always resisted very strongly the idea that the writer should be some sort of amateur in the theatre. I think it's a very practical job and I think you've got to know how to write parts for actors, you've got to know how to write sets that can be designed.

One of the best things about this job is that you work with other people. You learn to work with designers and lighting designers and costume designers and actors and directors and there's an interesting flexibility – you have to give them something and then they give you something and somewhere on the frontiers of that job some very interesting stuff goes on.

What's the best and worst thing about this job? The worst thing is that you're on your own for most of the time. The best thing is that when you're not on your own you're with really great people and the atmosphere is terrific compared with, say, working on movies where the writer is fairly unimportant.

I had a conscious strategy about my career as a writer: I wasn't going to write for television. So I haven't written for television and I decided that my strategy was that I would work in theatre and I was going to write for theatre and then after a while if things were going well I would try to get into films and that's what's happened. When you start writing you don't quite know what you're doing. It's quite possible you could write a good play but you don't usually know how or why you did it and I think it takes ten years before you can pretty much predict how the work will go.

My family used to make billiard tables for 120 years and writing for the theatre is like playing billiards, and writing for film is like playing snooker and anyone will tell you you can start playing billiards, which is quite a complicated game – you only play with three balls – and then you can play snooker, but you can't do it the other way round.

I'm just doing a film set in nineteenth-century Vienna and someone was saying, 'It's so incredible that you can characterise people in two or three speeches!' Well, yeah, that's theatre training, because you can't write a bad part because someone's got to do it every night, so I never write a part where someone's just a spear carrier: 'My Lord, here are letters for you.' I mean, I tend not to write small parts anyway because it's not economic, but if someone's going to come on and do this part every night there's got to be something in it that's good and I've applied that to the film world as well.

I always have more ideas than I have time to write and it's just a question of when you do them. You have to have a certain amount of time in your subconscious to develop ideas; people think writing plays is about writing dialogue – I spend hardly any of my time writing dialogue, I spend maybe a month a year writing dialogue, the rest of the time is thinking and planning.

One of the things about writing plays is you have to have a strategy about money, what's the plan – to live in relative poverty, which I did for quite a long time. Now, the thing about writing plays for money is that if you have a successful play at the Royal Court and you do, say, 60–70 per cent business, if it takes you a year to write, you would be earning less money than you would if you were a teacher – quite a lot less than you get being a teacher. So, I think it's important to have a strategy to approach this thing of making money, because a lot of writers have good careers for two or three years. If you set out to have a long career you have to do other things.

You also have to have an attitude towards how to keep sane – you go into a room on your own and you spend eight hours a day sitting at a desk and you have nothing to talk about. I spent eleven years at the Royal Court being Literary Associate, which meant that I was connected to a building. I went and talked to people, there were script meetings, there was gossip, you met people, the stuff of working life was happening to you, and that doesn't usually happen to you as a writer and it's a question of how you can cope with that.

I think you shouldn't do it the same way every time. I think it's very important you should have a sort of basic method – I started out as someone who wrote a lot of dialogue and then found out what the play was about. I now do it the other way round – I try to work out what the play is about. I have a very strong sense of structure now and I am confident that I can deliver the dialogue. Part of this method relies on the fact that I know that I can write the dialogue for a play in a week or a fortnight because I've done it before and know that if you trust that skill it won't let you down.

There's a great virtue in clarity but there's also a great virtue in not knowing where you're going and being instinctive.

CHAPTER 3

The director

A good director needs to have creativity and imagination, but there's much more to the job than that. The role of the modern director is a complex and varied one; they need the ability to communicate effectively with a diverse range of people, from the emotionally driven actor to the technically precise master carpenter. They should be willing to explore history, science, art, music, literature, costume, politics, geography, etc. – any subject that might be contained within the world of a play that they are to direct, in order to reach an understanding of the text.

A director must be able to cope under pressure and make several decisions at once. They must be able to motivate the people around them, and maintain a positive and encouraging atmosphere, even when they are tired and fed-up. They must be firm when required, but also sensitive to the needs of others. Finally, a director should have a desire to explore and ask questions, both of the world around them and the people in it.

Jobs in directing

Assistant director

Assistant directors (ADs) will typically be people who have just finished college and are in the early stages of their careers. As the name implies, they assist the director throughout the rehearsal period, but what that assistance is depends upon the director for whom you are working. For some ADs this may mean simply sitting in rehearsal and giving the director their feedback at the end of a session, or carrying out specific research and preparation tasks. Sometimes ADs will be asked to rehearse crowd scenes, or work with actors on a one-to-one basis to help with characterisations or on scenes in which they are struggling. Later in the process the AD might conduct line runs of the play, or rehearse the understudies. It's fair to say that the AD's role is that of dogsbody in terms of directing, but that this is the means by which they learn and observe experienced directors at work.

Freelance director

A freelance director is employed on a production-by-production basis by different theatre companies and they will usually have completed some training as well as spent time within a theatre company as an assistant. They will have gained enough experience and reputation to become independent professional directors for hire, and they will get work via a combination of suggesting productions to companies with whom they want to work, and being commissioned to direct by companies who are interested in their work. They will often undertake a broad variety of work, from rehearsed readings of new plays to directing youth theatres and community work, depending upon their interest.

Associate director

These are usually directors with significant reputations who are invited to become associated on a long-term basis with a particular theatre company. They are not involved in running the company, but their work will complement the artistic aims or emphasis of the company. The relationship is mutually beneficial, the theatre company gaining from being associated with a high-profile director while the director gains a permanent affiliation and the security that brings, as well as a commitment of work.

Artistic director

The artistic director is the head of a theatre company, whose role evolves in one of two ways. Some artistic directors have formed their own theatre companies early in their careers, usually in order to stage a certain type of work. They will rarely have worked for anyone else. Other artistic directors, especially those employed by large regional theatre companies in dedicated buildings, will be well-established, high-profile directors who are appointed to the post by the theatre's board of governors. Artistic directorship is the natural progression of the director's role, but it can be something of a poisoned chalice. The larger the theatre company the less time there is to be spent directing, as more time is spent running the company, and this is especially true where that company also runs a building. From an artistic point of view, the director shapes and communicates the theatre's artistic policy and aims, choosing the plays it stages and the directors who direct them. They will continue to direct themselves, but in many cases will manage just one production a year.

Production process

Of all the roles in the production of a play, the director's is the most arduous. The director is the first to start work and stays with the production for the longest time, until it opens and is up on its feet.

Pre-production

For the director, the production process begins with months of planning and preparation. More than 50 per cent of a director's work will be done before a single actor is cast, making preparation and pre-production one of the most critical aspects of her or his job.

Understanding the text

Directors choose a play – if they're lucky – because it excites, puzzles or challenges them. They become familiar with it, reading and rereading until they absorb it fully. During this process they may make notes, draw sketches, put together mood boards – each director has his or her own individual approach – and they will arrive at an overall concept, approach or interpretation of the play, which will define their production.

A summary of the director's key responsibilities

- Creating an interpretation of the play.
- Establishing a creative team.
- Casting actors.
- Choosing the performance configuration (proscenium, in the round, etc.).
- Managing the read-through and table-based sessions.
- Leading rehearsals.
- Blocking and movement.
- Talking to actors about character choices and supporting them in difficulty.
- Controlling the pace, rhythms and energy levels of the production.
- Liaising with production staff to prepare the production for opening night.
- Providing feedback and notes to cast and crew once the production is up and running.
- Ensuring the production remains fresh, especially during long runs.

All of these elements will be contained within the director's notes. Some directors' notes are like a journal recording their developing sense of the play, while others have notebooks that resemble scrapbooks full of pictures, research notes, poems, lyrics to songs, images from magazines – anything that has inspired them in relation to the play. At the end of this process, the director will have formed his or her own interpretation of the play.

This might be a checklist of the things a director will explore during their preparations.

Analysing a text

Context: What has just happened? What is about to happen?
Meaning: The controlling idea. Specific references or symbols. Line-by-line study.
Character: Who speaks? How much do we know about them? What are their genders? Their physical characteristics? The relationships? Their attitudes?
Language: Lyrical, conversational, heightened, use of imagery, choice of words and vocabulary.
Purpose: What was the playwright's intention in writing the play (different to the play's meaning)?
Sound: Rhythm, rhyme, how does the sound of the dialogue re-enforce meaning?
Tone: Serious, comic, ironic, angry, fearful, happy, romantic, sexual?

After the work on the text, the director begins to think about the nuts and bolts of the production – the space in which it will be staged, what sort of design they are interested in.

Types of staging

To a certain extent, the staging choices are limited by the type of theatre the play is to be performed in. However, increasingly directors are seeking innovative methods of changing the theatre space, particularly the traditional proscenium arch theatre that has dominated for the last two hundred years or so. They might cover over the stalls and put seats where the stage was to create a theatre-in-the-round, or make site-specific work that is seen by just a few people at a time. Whether taking this approach or staging in a more usual space, there are the six basic theatrical spaces.

Proscenium

As noted above, this form of stage has dominated theatre for close to two hundred years, and its legacy is still with us thanks to the rash of theatre-building during the late nineteenth century. The West End of London, and most towns and cities across the UK, had sumptuously adorned proscenium arch theatres built at this time, and most are now listed buildings, placing significant restrictions on the theatre companies who use them and preventing any change. The form consists of a deep square or rectangular stage that is fronted and surrounded by a 'frame' – in nineteenth-century theatres, literally a frame – an extravagant border as one might find on a picture, covered in gold and embellished with all manner of decoration. Its central conceit is that the audience are being allowed to look through an invisible fourth wall of what would be a closed room or space.

Thrust

The type of staging that Shakespeare would have been most familiar with, the thrust stage projects deep into the audience who surround it on three sides. The traditional thrust stage will have a large exit in the centre of its fourth side and this is the main entrance and exit. More recently, a hybrid form has evolved that pairs the thrust stage with a thin apron stage running across the back of the fourth side, offering exits left and right as well as at the centre. This form of staging derives from the structure of the courtyard inns, where travelling groups of actors often performed, a structure replicated in some of London's first permanent theatre buildings like the Curtain and the Globe. This staging is demanding on actors. Audiences are in front and to the side of them, and seated on different levels, so directors must consider the way that their actors focus and interrelate with one another to ensure that the audience is always included in the performance.

Amphitheatre

Often grouped with the thrust stage, there are in fact significant differences. The amphitheatre dates back to the time of ancient Greece where the auditorium and stage were constructed outdoors, initially from wood and then from stone. These theatres were huge, seating thousands of spectators. There are surviving Greek amphitheatres still in use today, mostly staging ancient Greek plays. The key features of the space are a flat circular performance space, edged by a narrow raised platform stage, behind which there is a tall façade with two doors in the centre, and the auditorium is a smooth continuous rake upwards from the stage, giving everyone a clear view of the stage. During the post-war period, when many towns and cities built new civic theatres, the amphitheatre became popular again for its 'democratic' layout; the audience were not segregated on different levels and everyone, on the whole, had a similar view of the stage. Because there is a gradual smooth sweep of the auditorium up and outwards this type of stage offers the actor good command of the audience, without having to focus on several levels.

Theatre-in-the-round
The theatre-in-the-round became popular during the radicalised theatre movement of the 1960s, when directors were searching for more inclusive and democratic forms of stage and auditorium relationship. In this configuration, the audience surround the action on all sides of either a circle or a square, with entrances/exits on the four 'compass points'. This sort of staging allows for little set, and requires particularly sophisticated blocking because actors will always have their back to a part of the audience.

Traverse
The traverse stage also evolved during the post-war radicalisation of theatre, and the desire to find different ways for an audience to 'see' a performance. Here the stage runs down the entire length of the space, at its centre, and the audience are seated on either side of it. In this way more spectators can be seated closer to the action. For directors and performers it's an unconventional playing space, which offers greater intimacy with the audience, while requiring careful positioning of actors.

Promenade
In many ways one of the oldest forms of staging, considering the 'stations' (stages) of the story of Christ as performed in churches during the early tenth and eleventh centuries, the form was reinvigorated during the 1960s. Much promenade theatre is site-specific, and stages a performance across a series of locations in one geographic place. Alternatively, the audience may be seated in the centre of the performance space while the action takes place around them, or the space will feature several stages on which scenes will take place at different times. This form of staging works particularly well for plays with a strong narrative drive.

Appointing the creative team
All of these aspects will have been considered during the preparation process. The next task for the director is to put together a creative team who can help realise the play. In general, this team will consist of set, costume, lighting and sound designers, an assistant director and a stage manager. Sometimes there will be just one designer who specialises in more than one aspect, such as set and costume, lighting and sound, and the stage manager and assistant director will often be assigned to the director by the theatre they are working for, rather than being selected or employed by the director, but this small nucleus of people sees the production through its next phase, the pre-production set-up.

Briefing the designer

Now that the director has the concept or interpretation for the production, they will meet with their designer to talk it through. Many directors establish relationships with a small group of designers early on in their careers, sometimes while still at college or university, and they will work with them on a regular basis thereafter. They will often share the same influences and approaches to making theatre, and the visuals and architectural style of the designer will chime with the director.

In their first discussion, then, the director will talk to the designer in the broadest terms about their reaction to the play, what they find significant in it, and any initial thoughts on the staging. If the play is set in a particular period or style they will discuss how they plan to approach this, and the designer, who will have already been working on the play independently, will share any thoughts and ideas they have had. These discussions will continue regularly throughout the pre-production period, until an overall visual concept is realised. From these conversations the designer will first make the sketches and then the model box, which will be presented to the cast on the first day of rehearsals.

Casting

One of the final tasks of the pre-production period is to cast the actors for the play, and how this occurs will depend on the context of the production. If a director is working for a theatre that is casting an acting company at the beginning of the season, they will take part in these auditions, seeing actors alongside the other directors, and then making the case for the actors they prefer when they gather to decide on their final choices. Otherwise, the director is, on the whole, free to cast for their show alone.

The cliché audition in which a nervous actor walks out to a single spotlight on the centre of the stage and delivers a pre-prepared speech to an anonymous director sitting in the darkness of the auditorium, ready to shout 'next' at the drop of the hat, is exactly that, a cliché, and thankfully relatively rare in today's theatre – it's not a good process for getting the best from people. However, there are many different approaches to the audition process, and each director will have his or her own. Some directors will cast 'to type', while others prefer to cast against it. Some like actors to prepare speeches for the audition, some like actors to read from the play being produced, while others prefer to hold workshops where they can see groups of actors and assess how they work together.

Large theatre companies have casting departments to assist in this process, and a director can outline the kind of performer they are after for each role and the casting director will gather together a range of actors to suit these needs. The director and the stage manager will then discuss how the audition process will be handled and the stage manager will liaise with the casting department to set the auditions up. Where there is no casting department a company will often employ a freelance casting director to do the same thing.

Auditions can take a number of forms. Some directors like to meet several actors with whom they will workshop parts of the play in different combinations, some will see actors in character groups. For example, if a director is casting Arthur Miller's *Death of a Salesman*, he or she may see actors in the family group the play focuses on – Mrs and Mrs Loman and their two grown-up sons.

The director's objectives in auditioning and casting are not just to get the right actor for the part, but to find actors that they can work with, who take direction well, have something to contribute to the production *and* are right for the part!

Some actors don't audition. Those that have reached a significant profile in the profession will be able to sell a show simply because they are in it. This gives an actor a considerable amount of clout and, as well as being offered a role, it allows them the opportunity to suggest productions to theatre companies for them to perform in.

Auditions over, the director will make their choices and the stage manager and the casting director will work together to notify agents, draw up contracts and send out scripts and information packs to those actors who have been successful.

This is the final stage of the pre-production process, although it may take place three or four months before the production proper begins. Everything is in place, however, and the individual parts of the team are all primed and ready to go. They come together on the first day of rehearsals for the meet and greet.

First rehearsal and the meet and greet
On the first day of rehearsal the director, the cast, the production team and as many theatre company staff as possible will meet informally over coffee to introduce themselves to each other. Known as a 'meet and greet', it serves to welcome the acting company and orient them to the building they'll be working in. The artistic director will welcome the new acting company and introduce the theatre's regular key staff, the play's director will talk about the production a little and then introduce those working on the play to the permanent company. This is particularly important for the actors, as many will have travelled away from their permanent home to be in the production and will stay 'in digs' for the duration of the rehearsals and performance. They won't necessarily know their fellow cast

members or the local area, and the permanent company can be an important bridge for them. The stage manager will then take the director and the cast on a tour of the building, instructing everyone on health and safety procedures, first-aid protocols and what to do in the event of a fire.

Creative team presentations

Following the meet and greet, the acting company move to the rehearsal room, which may be at the theatre, or a hall or room off-site. This will be their base for the rehearsal period. The director will introduce everyone to each other and talk in more detail about the production, what interests and inspires them about it and what they hope to achieve. The design team will then present the set model, and demonstrate how scenes will look, as well as displaying costume sketches. Any music that has been specially composed for the production will also be played.

All this is done at the first stage so that the actors and the other departments involved can see a visual representation of what they are working on, to hold in their minds until the actual production is on its feet.

Read-through

Seated in a circle and often round a table, the director will then lead the cast in a read-through of the play. They will not move any scene or make exits and entrances, they will simply speak the text out loud so that the whole company has a shared sense of the journey of the play. After weeks or months of preparation, the production proper has begun.

Rehearsals

The rehearsal room is where all the director's preparatory hard work pays off and is their opportunity to experiment with and explore the text using their skill and creativity, together with that of their actors. Some directors have a particular style or method of working, utilising the theories of specific practitioners such as Konstantin Stanislavsky, or Bertolt Brecht, while others will borrow from several theorists, or adapt their working methods according to the play they're directing. Some directors structure their rehearsals in great detail, beginning with physical warm-ups and games to aid the actor's concentration and focus them on the work that they are to do in the rehearsal room. They may follow this with some improvisation around the topic or scene that is to be rehearsed in that session, before moving on to work on the text itself. Other directors work on the text only – they may use games and improvisations at certain points, but not on a regular basis. The reality is that rehearsal systems are as unique as directors themselves. Some directors ask questions of their actors, as a way of prompting them to discover their characterisations and relationships; others do very little, stay silent and let the actors find their own way, only stepping in when the actors become stuck.

The majority follow a fairly loose pattern of working, in which emphasis is placed on understanding the text – especially important if working on period plays where the language patterns and vocabulary are not the same as we use today – exploring and establishing the relationships between the various characters in the play, and seeking out the meaning and emphasis in terms of the dramatic action of the play.

Proxemics

Proxemics means the position of people in relation to each other onstage. It works closely with characterisation and a relatively new science known as kinesics, which is the study of movement and gestures, and the meanings these can have in terms of personality or character.

The position of people in any group is significant – it tells you a lot about their relationships – and this knowledge can be used when exploring spatial relationships onstage. Where a character stands and with whom or away from whom all has a relevance to what is being conveyed to an audience, in terms of the relationships being established. This should also be considered in terms of the character's relationship to the physical space he or she is in.

Simply by arranging bodies in a physical space, a director can imply connections, weaken or strengthen the relationships between characters, create tension and heighten or suppress mood and atmosphere. By arranging characters differently within a space, different things are implied.

This awareness is combined practically in the process known as 'blocking'. Once a fairly perfunctory process of telling actors where to enter and exit and where to move onstage, today's directors take a more holistic approach, exploring movement as part of a journey the actors go on as their characters develop.

Blocking

Traditionally, the stage space is divided up into sections and referred to in shorthand, for ease of use by actors and directors and simple recording by stage management. The layout is assigned from the audience's point of view.

Movement will almost always upstage dialogue and stage movement is a powerful creator of meaning. In most twentieth-century and contemporary plays this movement onstage is justified by character motivation or intention. It is the job of the director to marry the character motivation that the actor feels is appropriate with the visual needs of the scene.

A director needs to consider sightlines – that is the view from different parts of the auditorium when watching the play. If the audience can't see key moments of the play they won't understand it. Blocking makes sense of the relationships between characters and helps create focus for the audience, showing them which action in a scene is important.

Planning a rehearsal

Whatever the approach, for the next two to three weeks the director and cast will embark on an adventure, breaking down the play to explore it for meaning, subtext and motivation. While each actor is on a personal journey of exploration with their character, the director must retain an overview and draw them all into a coordinated whole that will make sense to an audience and entertain them too.

Production meetings

The production team, which comprises the designers, a stage manager and other personnel as required, such as a composer, a movement director, a vocal coach or a puppeteer, meet regularly with the director to discuss the progress of the production, agree deadlines and resolve any problems that occur. A director does this in addition to the rehearsal commitment, often having to meet at the end of a long day of rehearsal, or in lunch hours.

Run-throughs

By the third week of rehearsal, actors will have learnt their lines and begun to run through the play on a regular basis. The director does this gradually, building scenes, then sequences of scenes, and finally running the whole play, so that actors get a sense of the overall rhythm of the play and how to pace themselves through it. For the director this is a testing time. It is the last opportunity to alter or revise any aspect of the production and the point at which they can gauge whether what they set out to achieve at the start has been realised.

Technical week

In the week before the production is due to open to the public, the play moves from the rehearsal room into the theatre or studio where it is to be performed. This phase is known variously as production week or technical week and is the point where all the various departments who have been working on the play come together, under the supervision of the director, the production manager and the stage manager.

Get-in
Over the preceding weekend any set from a previous play will be taken down or struck and the set for the new play will be got in, hence the term 'get-in'. The set will be installed and the lights will be rigged, focused and plotted on to a manual or computerised lighting board. Music and sound effects will be loaded into whichever system the theatre uses, and speakers and basic sound levels checked. The director's role in this process is minimal, but with the completion of the get-in and fit-up that changes.

Technical rehearsal
The technical rehearsal is the coming together of the two worlds of the director, the one they have been supervising in the rehearsal room and the one they have been supervising via production meetings. Seated in the auditorium, the director watches while the stage manager runs the show 'cue to cue', that is, skipping through the text and running only the sections in which there is some sort of technical cue, whether that be for lighting, sound, costume or scene change. The stage manager is in charge and will stop the technical run as and when things don't work, are wrong or need reworking, although they may be prompted in this by the director, the designer or one of the other creatives. It's a lengthy and often frustrating process as last-minute hitches occur and props, scenery or effects don't quite do what they are supposed to.

There is a great potential for error and one of the key jobs of the director in this context is to maintain a sense of positive calm, methodically working through each problem that occurs, all the time ensuring that the integrity of the production is not compromised.

Dress rehearsals
The technical rehearsal is followed by the dress rehearsals, of which there are usually two. The first is somewhat fondly referred to as a 'stagger-through' as it is the first time the whole play is put together with all its technical elements and run as though an audience were present. It's rare for this to go without a hitch. The second dress rehearsal tends to be much closer to what the audience will see each evening, but on very complicated shows, technical difficulties can mean that the opening of a show is delayed until problems can be

fixed. No director wants to open his or her show until it's as good as it can be.

The dress rehearsal is a demanding period for the director, as it is the culmination of their artistic vision. They are wrestling with a string of questions, some focused on the creative side of the work – Have they got it right? Does the reality look like the world they imagined? Have the actors fully understood their characters and inhabited them? – others concerned with practical matters – Will the revolve work in Scene four? Is the lighting for the opening too dark? – but most of all, have they served the playwright and the audience by creating a thought-provoking and entertaining work of art?

Previews

The play opens with little fanfare or fuss for a series of preview performances, which are often dress rehearsals to which audiences pay to come. It gives the director an opportunity to test their production in front of an audience to ensure that it works, the pace is correct, the characterisations 'true' and the meaning and action of the play clear. They continue to make copious notes, which they will give to the actors either immediately after curtain down, or prior to the performance the following day. They might also call short rehearsals of scenes they want to rework, change or tighten. All this is to get the production in the best possible shape for the play's official opening night.

Opening night

The official opening night of a production is also usually press night, the point at which theatre critics attend and review the production. It is an anxiously anticipated event and one with some sense of occasion. Well-known celebrities and performers are often invited to opening nights, as are local dignitaries such as mayors, councillors, funders and sponsors. The director is on duty both backstage, reassuring nervous actors, and front of house, speaking to journalists and guests alike. The director will watch the show, often from the lighting box, continuing to make notes and trying to gauge the audience's and critics' reaction.

The run

Once the play is in production, the stage manager supervises it on a day-to-day basis and the director's job is done. Unless they are a permanent member of the theatre company, in which case they may be moving straight into the next production, they will go elsewhere for their next job. However, where one is present, the assistant director will watch the show regularly during its run to keep an eye on it, look out for things that aren't working and check that actors haven't altered their performances so radically that the play has lost its sense. Some directors will also drop in unannounced to check on the production and give notes or advice to the cast and keep them on their toes!

Get-out
Where possible, a director will try to return for the final night of the run. As a freelance director they will often have gone into rehearsals for their next production, but they will try to take time out to congratulate the cast and crew for all their hard work.

Once the set, costumes and technical equipment have all been taken down, or 'struck', and removed from the theatre – got out – some companies have cast parties onstage. Other companies will hold their parties at the rehearsal space, while others will hire a separate external venue for the occasion. In smaller companies with smaller casts, the group might opt to go for a meal together instead, but it is traditional to find some way to mark the end of the production before everyone disperses.

Finding out more

Braun, Edward, *The Director and the Stage*, A & C Black, 2003
Brook, Peter, *The Empty Space*, Penguin, 1983
Clark, Max Stafford, *Letters to George*, Nick Hern Books, 2001
Irvin, Polly, *Directing for the Stage*, Roto Vision, 2003
McCaffery, Michael, *Directing a Play*, Phaidon Press, 1994
Mitter, Shomit, ed., *Fifty Key Theatre Directors*, Routledge, 2005
Taylor, Don, *Directing Plays*, A & C Black, 1996
Vaughn, Stuart, *Directing Plays: A Working Professional's Method*, Longman Publishing Group, 1992

Getting started

Michael Boyd

I think the first stage was probably cutting out Christmas cards and putting them on pieces of wire and making my own version of a toy theatre, with my friends, and, quite fancy, putting light bulbs in and so on, and doing shows for people. When I was nine I wrote a play about Sherlock Holmes and I played Sherlock Holmes and my best friend played Watson.

I didn't go to the theatre a lot. And then at university, the University of Edinburgh, just doing a lot of, again, the usual undergraduate work, treading the tightrope between the risk of academic failure and the excitement of doing work in the theatre. And I suppose there came a point where I very much enjoyed acting, I very much enjoyed directing, and I very much enjoyed writing, towards the end of university. And I didn't really know which way I wanted to jump.

I went to the Soviet Union in 1979/80. I went to the [Malaya Bronnaya] Theatre in Moscow. So a very formative thing was seeing rehearsals at the Malaya Bronnaya, seeing a read-through last three weeks, seeing rehearsals that lasted six months to a year, as opposed to the customary three to four weeks in the British theatre. And the depth of enquiry that was involved in their work was hugely influential. And also the kinaesthetic excitement that they sought in their work. There was of course the text, but there was an entire event that was a theatre show, that was plastic as well as verbal. And the two in harmony, at its best, in a very exciting way.

So often as an assistant director you make the tea, and I got to do ten shows. It was fabulous.

I quite enjoy the extraordinary intensity of the rehearsal room, which I just emerged from yesterday on *Richard the Third.* That kind of manic obsession with one central object, which is the show. And then coming out of that. The very healing sanity of the rest of the world, and things that are perhaps not quite as intense, but just as important. It's quite a balance, it's quite healthy.

It's very hard to get practice as a director. Because getting actors together is potentially very expensive and putting shows on, even with like-minded people, who are therefore happy to work for next to nothing, can still be expensive because you're not being paid. I would say get yourself into a position where there are the resources, potentially, for you to do as many shows as possible.

Beg, borrow, steal tickets to go and see shows that you've heard are good. Bad work can be instructive to watch but good work is even more instructive.

I think there is something about allowing yourself to benefit from the community of like-minded souls, which is a nice thing that can happen at university or at college.

Nicholas Hytner

I think in the end as artistic director you're responsible for everything that goes on here: choosing the plays we do, finding the new plays, the new voices, finding the people who are going to write the new plays. So, in brief, just choosing the repertoire is the big job.

And then beyond that? You've got to make sure that when you've chosen the rep that it gets done as well as possible. So that's about finding the directors and working with them to make sure that they find the best designers, the best musicians and the best actors. So, just to keep summing up, you've got policy, repertoire and making sure that the repertoire is done as well as possible.

Even the state of the carpet and whether the banners outside are shining or not in the end comes within my remit. It's all part of what face the National Theatre is turning to the world, how good the sandwiches are, the lot, you can get involved in everything.

I work harder than I did before I was the director of the NT, and maybe I direct a little less and I certainly don't, couldn't, wouldn't want to direct a big movie or a West End musical. I direct twice a year, here, and that's about it, although occasionally I allow myself a little sabbatical doing something else. But twice a year is actually kind of enough. It means that there are certain things which I can't do, and over the last three years plays have come along which I would have dearly loved to have directed but I can't.

You don't need to be a director of plays to be the director of a theatre – an actor could run a theatre, a writer could run a theatre. It's become habitual now for directors to run theatres for all sorts of reasons, some good, some bad. But you know, more and more now, actor managers are coming back and I think that's a very, very good idea.

The best directors don't so much impose their personality on the play as release something that is in the play to its greatest extent.

The reason I think that directors of plays have tended to be quite successful at running theatres is that I think many of us work by being able to take a step back from the individual project, from the play, and to make sure that everybody is working productively and together. Mostly, it's not about saying this is my vision, this is how the play is going to be. It's mostly about having at the core a vision – pulling everybody together and getting the best out of them. When I work with a designer it's not very often that I say this is exactly how every scene of this play is going to look, it's more 'I have a few ideas, what are your ideas? Change my ideas if you like.' It's the same working with actors, musicians ... that approach to the theatre, which is having a core commitment, a core passion but wanting everybody else to work to their absolute fullest extent and to stretch their imaginations to the limit, and to changing each other's ideas all the time, but in the end pull it together to one central thing. That's what you do when you're directing a play and running a theatre. So, that's why so often theatres are run by directors. Actors can do that as well, of course they can, of course they can.

Young directors think it's all about bossing people around – it's absolutely not about bossing people around. What it's about is listening to everybody and making sure that everybody feels they are being given the framework to do their absolute best work.

You need to try and do everything else. I realised I was a terrible actor and a terrible writer, but I was passionately interested in the theatre, completely possessed by it. If you go to college or university, make sure you get involved with thinking about how to sell the seats, designing the poster, or getting someone to design the poster and making sure it's stuck up in the right places. There's no job that you shouldn't feel excited by. In an ideal world, training courses for directors should be training courses in everything except directing. Do everything is my advice.

When you create something that is true, has real life in it, isn't just an acted, artificial, performed show-offy facsimile of it, but real life, those moments of superior truth, truth that is truer than mundane reality, that's what's really exciting.

Rachel Kavanaugh

There is no substitute for being in that rehearsal room, first as an assistant and then doing it. It's about how you run that room and how you translate those words or those ideas on the page into a piece of theatre, and you can theorise as much as you like about it but if you can't get your creative team and your actors to realise that vision then it's no good.

I learnt a huge amount from assisting. That was my training, if one wants to use that word, because I worked with a lot of different directors and I learnt both positively and negatively. That's valuable! There's always something you can learn from everybody, I think.

For me, the most exciting, creative moments come in rehearsal when suddenly I'll get fired up about a scene, or a moment or a relationship, and want to work it or explore it – What if we do this? What if we do that? Oh, I've suddenly thought how to solve that moment. That, for me, feels sort of actively creative if you like.

I don't have a clear methodology in that way but I have a series of events that happen when I get offered a play or an idea comes up. I tend to know pretty quickly when I read something whether it's something I want to do, and I've learnt, as much as is possible, to trust that rather emotional response to something and not try and reason myself one way or another. It's generally that old thing of just reading it. Then I would talk to a designer quite soon. I find that a very helpful way of getting to know the play better, of thinking about it just in another way, which isn't just reading it in your head off the page.

I used to do more games and exercises in rehearsals than I do now, that's all gone away a bit really, now I'm pretty straight with what I do in rehearsal. I will always explore something just in terms of what's written on the page first. But, in my experience, actors, there's a limit to how long they want to sit down.

What you need to find is a way of illuminating and entertaining. I think there needs to be a positive decision about the play which conveys an enthusiasm about it to an audience.

I think it's [directing] a bit like hostessing a rather marvellous party in a way; that sounds very trite, but it's just about keeping the energy in the room positive and good. I mean, people always remark about the amount of laughter in my rehearsals and it's not a conscious thing, I just think it's a very healthy thing.

The same skills are brought to bear being artistic director – the ones I'm talking about such as communication – it's a kind of extension of directing. You're not just running a room now, you're running a building, it's just bigger.

It's a very steep learning curve in terms of many aspects of the job, in terms of relationships with funding organisations, staff management, budgets. All that stuff you don't have to worry about when you're a freelance director. But I think it's very important for me that I don't do less directing. So now I'm basically doing two jobs when before I was doing one.

CHAPTER 4

The actor

Acting is one of the most glamorous and high-profile fields of professional theatre, and while it may be true to say that the best actors make it look effortless, that's not to say they haven't worked hard to make it appear so. However, for all the glamour and celebrity of those we see on the stages of our leading theatres, acting is a difficult career to pursue, and though it's something of a cliché to point out that many more actors are unemployed than are employed, it is also a truism and a cliché that it's a profession that attracts people with passion and dedication who are prepared to chase their dreams to the point of distraction. It is often said that the real difference between the successful working actor and the star-struck wannabe is the ability to see acting as a job, assess one's strengths and weaknesses within it, and then to make career choices accordingly.

While it is possible to become an actor without any formal training, such instances are rare. Most actors become interested in performing early on, and many get involved in drama at school, participating in school plays, joining youth theatres and taking drama qualifications as part of their GCSEs. Some young people decide to commit themselves very early on and attend stage schools, where the traditional school curriculum is balanced with drama-related classes such as singing, dancing, voice and movement.

The majority of performers train at a recognised drama school or take an established university drama degree. Entry to most of these courses is via audition and interview – the first of many occasions where an actor's success or failure is judged by a brief audition. At drama school, as at stage school, the focus is on practical technique as well as the acquisition of theory. Once admitted, the schedule is punishing, with classes starting at nine in the morning and continuing until six or seven o'clock at night, later when students are involved in productions. There are classes in dance, movement, voice and acting techniques as well as the study of text and forms of combat, physical theatre and maybe circus skills. University courses will differ from those at drama schools because students will also be studying for a formal academic degree. This necessarily means that there is more written and research content in the degree course. Some drama schools and courses take a specialist approach, usually drawn from the theories of one or other leading theatre practitioner or a specific theatre technique, such as Brecht or devising. At the end of their three-year course, actors take part in graduation performances to which theatrical agencies are invited and the scrum is on to get yourself an agent.

Theatre work is held by many actors to be the most satisfying experience both in terms of the rehearsal process – the opportunities to explore characterisation and meaning – and the camaraderie that develops between the cast and crew – working on a show together for several months. Most of all, actors appreciate the opportunity to perform for a live audience, gauging their reactions as the play unfolds – an experience not afforded the film or television actor. However, the greatest drawback to live theatre is that of all the work available to an actor it is the least well paid. Actors are self-employed; sole traders who don't earn salaries or get the benefits associated with full-time employment, such as holiday and sickness pay or pension schemes. It is not surprising therefore that most agents, and actors themselves, however much they love live performance, often pursue film and TV work over that in theatre.

Jobs in acting

Lead actor

Lead actors are usually spotted early in their careers, by scouts who visit drama schools to watch end-of-year and graduation productions. Occasionally, a lead actor might be discovered through the general audition process, or be a young actor, who as he or she gains experience, shows the potential to play lead roles. What makes a leading actor is harder to define. In film and television it's more straightforward, usually helped by good looks and photogenic features, or the fact that the dimensions and physical make-up of the actor's face transfer very well on to film – hence the phrase 'the camera loves you'.

In the theatre, there is less emphasis on the actor's appearance. Many of today's leading theatre actors do not have model good looks, but what they will have are great vocal skills, presence, the ability to inhabit the character and make it believable, and the maturity, even when still quite young, to take on major roles and make them their own. These actors are the ones who play the great roles – Juliet, Hamlet – and define them for a generation or an entire age. Today, Laurence Olivier's Henry V is still talked about, though very few remain alive who will have seen the original theatre performance.

Character actor

The character actor has a much less glamorous effect on their audiences, their impact being made more traditionally over time. Character actors are those who early in their careers discover the chameleon-like ability to play a great variety of roles, each time subsuming themselves into the part until they are almost unrecognisable. Traditionally, such actors also have the ability to play a range of ages, even when young.

In the past, there was a sense that the character actor was what you became because you couldn't make it as a lead, but increasingly young actors are making the choice to pursue 'character' roles. Good character actors are rarely out of work – a fair number of our leading character actors have made successful careers in American movies. Many character actors build up a significant reputation across decades, and become much-loved household names through diverse work on stage, television and film.

Ensemble/company actor

Since the revolutionary alternative theatre movement of the 1960s, there have been a number of niche companies that have had a great impact on theatre and achieved a very high profile – companies such as Complicite, Kneehigh and, in America, Steppenwolf and the Wooster Group. They are founded by like-minded individuals – actors, directors and writers – who are bound together by an idea of theatre or a particular approach. Actors who work in such companies rarely audition. Instead they develop organically, with their friends and colleagues, as the company's ideas and methods develop. To subsidise their work with the company, these actors may sometimes work outside the group, often on commercial projects. These companies often develop at university, college or drama school.

Physical and devising actor

As with those actors who choose to become part of a particular company, some actors decide to specialise in specific forms of theatre performance, largely because they enjoy an aspect of the process. This is especially true of actors who specialise in physical and devised theatre. Physical theatre as a movement has its roots in the work of Meyerhold, a pupil of Stanislavsky, as well as a number of other traditions from commedia to kabuki. It saw a resurgence during the post-war years when young theatre-makers looked outside the established process, seeking something fresh and new, and a number of practitioners evolved methodologies that were not tied to script or traditional naturalistic acting techniques. Actors who work in these forms will often take specialist training, usually after, or in reaction to, a traditional training at drama school. It is unusual to find actors who specialise in physical or devised theatre from the outset, largely because it is a form that is not widely taught at school other than in a rudimentary fashion. Physical theatre requires particular skills, as does devised theatre.

Actor-teacher

The actor-teacher is another evolution from the alternative theatre movement, when actors took teaching degrees in order to develop work through theatre-in-education (TIE) companies. These toured schools across the country using theatre to introduce young people to different ideas and aspects of what they needed to study. This form of theatre dwindled in the 1980s when many TIE companies had their funding cut as part of the political arts policies of the period. However, recently there has been a renewal of TIE work in schools, as teachers recognise the value of drama in conveying difficult concepts. Most young people today are quite visually astute, exposed as they are from an early age to a wide diversity of visual stimuli, from TV, films and the Internet to computer and console games.

It is beyond a book such as this to cover the production process for all the performance forms mentioned above in any depth. So, here, we'll explore the traditional text-based production process, but the bibliography given at the end of the chapter lists titles that give more in-depth information about different production approaches.

Production process

Pre-production

For the actor, the production process begins with being cast, either as part of a company, or for a specific part in one production. In commercial productions the usual practice is to cast one actor to perform one role, or occasionally to double a couple of parts. In the subsidised sector, however, there are a number of different approaches, ranging from theatres that cast a company who will take roles in a season of plays, to theatres that operate a repertory system but cast actors for each show rather than a whole season. Some companies audition for long-term members where the content of the audition will rely more heavily on skills than on the delivery of speeches.

Agents, casting directors and departments

Before an actor can audition, he or she has to reach the attention of the casting director or department, and the most conventional way to do this is to employ a theatrical agent. I use the term 'employ' pointedly, because it is worth noting that the actor employs the agent, not the other way round. For young actors it can often be a scrabble to find an agent, and there is a disproportionate hierarchy of agencies who see themselves as an elite. Many young actors feel they have failed if they are not taken on by one of these 'A-list' agents. However, the truth is an actor needs an agent who will get them work – it's better to be the most important client of a small or solo agent, keen to get you the best work, rather than one of many actors represented by a junior agent in a large firm for whom you are a lower priority than some of their more established clientele. It is an accepted fact that actors switch agents regularly – often as their careers improve and develop – and any young actor who finds their star in the ascendant will suddenly find themselves being courted by high-profile agents who showed no interest in them at their drama school's graduation show. Most importantly, an actor must find an agent who understands them and their work, can advise them and help develop their career, and will respect the sort of work the actor wants to do and help find it.

Theatre companies looking to audition for productions or seasons issue casting notices, and these notices go to agents as well as specialist casting publications such as 'PCR' ('Professional Casting Report'). The agent will then submit a series of candidates to the company's casting director for consideration, and the preferred candidates will be invited to audition. This process is facilitated by the actor's headshot and CV, and it's the headshot that is the actors' chief calling card. Actors usually have to arrange their own headshots and there are a number of photographers who specialise in such work and are found in the pages of *Contacts*. Good headshots are hard to achieve and are worth their weight in gold as they are often the sole means of achieving an audition. They should be straightforward and not over-complicated or 'arty'. The function of a headshot is to let whoever is casting see your physical appearance, or 'look'. This may seem arbitrary and unfair but it's the way this process works.

Some theatre companies have some sort of casting director or department, while others employ freelance casting directors to do the job for them. The casting director's role is to meet the casting needs of the production's director, who will have formed a sense of the sort of world they want to create in their production and hence the type of actor they are looking for for each role. This is a more complex job when casting a company who will take part in several plays across a season. Here the emphasis will be on finding actors with a range of playing ages, skills and abilities, and not just the right look for an individual production.

It is the casting director or department who will compare the submitted headshots with the director's list of requirements, select the appropriate actors and invite them to audition. Casting preparations are often made well before the start of the rehearsal process – anything from three months to a year where internationally renowned actors are concerned, to ensure their availability.

Types of audition
The audition itself can take many forms depending on the director or company involved and the type of production being staged.

Open auditions
These are most often used to audition for musical theatre, and are the sort of thing commonly seen in films, where an actor moves centre stage into a solo spotlight to perform for an unseen and all-powerful director sitting in the shadows of the auditorium, or where the dancer is asked to join a group of dancers onstage to be mercilessly put through their paces by a relentless choreographer. While this certainly does happen, in straight theatre productions it is the least successful way of finding suitable performers.

One-to-one auditions
These are where a director will meet with an actor individually, talk to them informally to see if they get on, and ask them to read sections of the play, often getting them to play a scene in a variety of styles. In this way a director can gauge how 'directable' an actor is, and what range of abilities they have.

Workshop auditions
These involve a large group of actors, usually assembled for a whole day, who engage in a range of activities with the director, from warm-ups and games exercises to work on the given text. The same process as the one-to-one audition is at work here; the director is evaluating each actor's abilities, but is also looking to see how the actors work with each other and what sort of 'team' they make.

Group auditions
These will usually involve several actors who together might make up a cast. The director will ask the actors to read scenes, swapping them into different roles to see what sort of combination might work effectively in the final casting.

Readings are often ways of casting new plays. An audience will be invited to hear part or all of the play read, and it will be semi-staged and worked by the director to see if the actors chosen are right for it. It may be several months before the production is actually staged, and if cast an actor must decide whether they want to accept the role and therefore limit their availability.

Most auditions aim to be relaxed and relatively informal. A director will want to know what other work an actor has done, as well as how they relate to the other actors at the audition and what they think of the play itself. Above all, a director is trying to gauge the actor's abilities, what type of performance they feel they might be able to extract from them, whether this ties in with their ideas for the play and, most important, whether the director feels a rapport with the actor.

Once an actor is cast, their agent will negotiate a contract depending on the role and where the play is being staged. Equity, the actors' trade union, and a number of other state-recognised bodies have determined set rates of pay and standard contracts for actors according to the status of the theatre and the type of production being staged. Where an actor is expected to tour or be away from home for any length of time, the actor will also be paid 'subsistence', an additional amount to cover their living expenses. The theatre company will send the actor an information pack containing a script, details of the production schedule, a date for the all-important first rehearsal as well as a range of other information they feel will help, from directions on how to find the theatre to a 'digs list' – details of local accommodation frequently used by visiting actors, local services, etc. It is very often the case that many regional theatre companies hold auditions in London because it has the largest population of actors.

First rehearsal

This is the point at which the acting ensemble comes together for the first time as a group. At this rehearsal they also meet the rest of the creative team and the staff of the theatre company they are working for.

Once introductions have been made, the cast and crew will sit in a circle or round a table and read through the play. The function of the read-through for the cast is to hear their voices together for the first time, and to move the script off the page and into a more three-dimensional reality. Some actors will have already formulated a characterisation in their heads, while others will deliver a neutral characterisation, waiting to see what evolves in rehearsal. The director will often explain their interpretation of the play and any important themes or aspects they want to explore. Where the company has a specific methodology or approach to text and rehearsals, this will also be explained. Then the creative team will discuss the design elements of the play, beginning with the set design, then followed by costume, light and sound. Stage management will make sure that all the actors' contact details are correct and their accommodation needs are taken care of and, where appropriate, take the actors on a tour of the building. Depending on the schedule, some companies will begin rehearsals straight away, while others will start formal rehearsals the following morning.

Rehearsals

Rehearsal techniques, as we have already seen, can vary from director to director, and some will have a very formal method while others will take a more relaxed approach. The rehearsals will usually be a combination of determining practicalities – where actors come on, go off and move to in between, which props they use and where they will get them from – to discussions about character, motivation and their interrelationships.

Some directors will begin each rehearsal with a formal warm-up and improvisation work aimed at preparing actors for the text they are to work on during that session; others leave actors to carry out their own warm-ups and focus mostly on the text, perhaps using improvisation only if they feel there is a particular problem to overcome. The key for the actor is flexibility and an awareness of their own process. Actors must be adaptable, and those with very strong feelings about the method in which they wish to work usually only audition for companies who work the same way. As rehearsals progress, the actor is working with the others in the cast to explore the text for its meaning and trying to find ways to express that meaning in the characterisation they are creating. Each actor's approach will be unique.

During the rehearsal period, actors can also expect to be called for costume or wig fittings; they might be asked to go on shopping trips with the head of wardrobe or other members of the technical team.

Books down

Books down is the point in rehearsal when actors should have learnt their lines. From now on, no scripts are allowed and the DSM will prompt actors who forget their lines.

Technical week

Technical week can be a tense time for the performer, as nerves and anxiety build regarding the upcoming performance, opportunities to rehearse reduce and focus shifts on to the technical elements of the play. The director is occupied elsewhere, and some actors might organise their own 'speed runs' of the play – a run-through of the lines of the play from beginning to end, at speed, as a way of maintaining a sense of readiness. Where the director has concerns, he or she might ask an assistant director to go through key scenes with actors, who also expect to attend final costume fittings, as well as carrying out their marketing duties by giving interviews to local or national press and attending photo calls.

Dress rehearsals

A dress rehearsal is both exhilarating and nerve-racking for the actor as it is the culmination of all their hard work, as well as an opportunity to bring all their skill and creativity together in their performance, at full energy, for the first time. There are usually two dress rehearsals, the first known as the 'stagger-through', largely because it can be difficult, being the first time the whole production operates as it will for each performance, and the aim is that each show runs to time.

Previews

The preview performances allow the actors to test their performances in front of an audience, before the pressure of press night, giving them a chance to make adjustments where scenes or characterisations are not quite working. Actors have an instinctive sense of when an audience is engaged in what they are seeing, and when they are not, and they use this judgement to help them in their performances. The director will watch each preview and afterwards everyone will gather for the director's notes. The director will often arrange additional work on a scene for the following day, prior to the evening performance, all with the aim of improving the production.

The previews offer the cast and crew a chance to work themselves in, and after two or three performances everyone has – hopefully – begun to relax enough for things to flow smoothly.

Opening night

Opening night, usually the show's press night, can be a glamorous affair, with an audience of invited guests, dignitaries and sponsors along with loyal and regular audience members. Some actors will invite friends and family to the opening night for moral support, while others prefer to be left alone to focus on their performance. Traditionally, in the West End of London, a first-night party followed the performance where everyone had the opportunity to let their hair down as they waited for the next day's papers, and their reviews, to be published. More recently, and away from the commercial West End, this is rarely the case. Critics rarely all attend a performance on the same night any more, and some companies might have to wait three or four days between a critic seeing a production and the review appearing in the paper. Local papers are often published once a week, while web-based news sources can have their review online in a matter of minutes.

The run
Each actor approaches the run of a play in his or her own way. Few rise early, given that they work late into the night, and while some prefer to spend their day quietly, preparing themselves for the evening performance, others take classes, visit the gym and see friends. Most actors like to arrive at the theatre one and a half to two hours before the performance. Where complex make-up or costuming are needed it may require them to be there earlier.

Some companies hold formal warm-up sessions which they expect the whole cast to attend, while others leave actors to do their own individual warm-up. The latest an actor can arrive at the theatre is the stage manager's half-hour call.

Actors receive calls from the stage manager over the backstage relay, telling them when they are needed onstage, and while some actors are happy to sit in their dressing room reading or doing crosswords, others prefer to be close to the action and will sit in the wing space.

After the performance, some actors prefer to go straight home, while others will go out together to socialise and this will be the pattern for the duration of the run.

Get-out and the last night
On the night of the final performance the actor will perform as usual. It's often a show that their friends and family will come to, and spirits are usually high. Many actors distribute thank-you cards and gifts to members of the cast and crew. Once the performance is over, the actor will clear their dressing room or dressing area and ensure that costumes are returned to maintenance wardrobe, while personal props are given back to stage management. Usually the director will return for the final night's show and the whole company might go out together for a meal, or the theatre might throw a last-night party.

Finding out more

Berry, Cicely, *Text in Action*, Virgin Books, 2001
Boal, Augusto, *Games for Actors and Non Actors*, Routledge, 2002
Callow, Simon, *Being an Actor*, revised edn, Picador, 2003
Donnellan, Declan, *The Actor and the Target*, Theatre Communications Group, 2002

Dunmore, Simon, *An Actor's Guide to Getting Work*, A & C Black, 2007
Hodge, Alison, *Twentieth Century Actor Training*, Routledge, 2002
Johnstone, Keith, *Impro for Storytellers*, Theatre Arts, 1999
Walter, Harriet, *Other People's Shoes – Thoughts on Acting*, Nick Hern
    Books, 2004

Getting started

Simon Russell Beale

I remember very clearly the first time I was asked to read Shakespeare – I was about eight, it was *Julius Caesar*, why is it always *Julius Caesar*? The headmaster who was taking the class gave me ten out of ten. I suppose I became interested in theatre at prep school, but then at senior school I had a master – one of the great teachers, you know. I was well on the way to being a doctor because that's what my parents did, and he switched paths for me really, he was an extraordinary man.

I would say if you get a chance to go to university, go to university because there's no hurry. That's the awful thing about being eighteen, isn't it? You want it. It's fine, you've got time, twenty-one isn't going to make much difference. That three years at university was an incredibly valuable time for me. I think some sort of training, whether it's university or whether it's a drama school, is vital.

I don't believe in that thing of 'oh I've got something else to fall back on'. I don't really see the point. I think it's a horrible way to do anything. You do it because you love it. If you have something else that you love, do it, train in it. If you want to do it do it. Yes, 90 per cent of actors are always out of work all the time, but 10 per cent are in work and you might be one of that 10 per cent who's always in work. I hate giving advice but I say be wary of making yourself miserable by doing something you don't really believe in!

I never anticipated being a member of the RSC, or indeed the National, at any point really, at the beginning. I worked mostly on new writing with Jenny Killick, who ran the Traverse, and then I went to the Royal Court and did something which I have never done since and probably would never do now, which is to say to the director, 'I really think I should do this part because it's me.' And bless him, Bill Gaskill obviously thought, OK, I'll give it to him. And then I got the call from the RSC. I think I realised that I've always been a person who gives his heart to institutions of one kind or another, I don't think I'm a natural freelancer at all.

When you get to know a part very well, or your particular version of that part, in the case of Hamlet, very well, then there does come such a release and it usually happens when you're tired and actually not trying too hard and it just comes out. That's a wonderful feeling.

From about three o'clock I have to be in the theatre and people think it's really weird but I have a rest . . . I couldn't rush in at six-thirty for a show at seven-thirty. I just couldn't do it, I would find it really distressing, and the very few occasions that I've been rehearsing all day and performing in the evening it's always been a little bit of a problem.

The least appealing thing is the hour before the show starts when you've already done two hundred. Actually, I'll be honest, the hour before the show full stop. I don't like the hour before the show, I find it . . . I still get nervous and I still get tense. Long runs are tricky, there's no question about it.

The most appealing thing . . . well, there are lots. I mean, I think actors are very nice people and I have very rarely met horrible actors. I think for the most part the people I've worked with are bright, inquisitive, switched-on people and I think that probably the greatest joy of all is being in the company of people who are that receptive to the world around them. Concomitant with that is the fact that, especially with new work, I love this thing that for six months you have to do astrophysics or for six months you have to do moral philosophy or for six months you have to do astronomy or for six months you have to do late-nineteenth-century Russia, so there's always some intellectual challenge in whatever play you do and I think that's fascinating.

What's lovely about the job? Well, you know about the intensity of one's working relationships . . . the number of people I've worked with who I don't see very much and yet ten years later I would probably be able to walk into a rehearsal room and pick it up again.

This inquisitiveness is actually very important. I think the actors I've met are some of the most inquisitive people I know.

Mike Shepperd

I tried the business in London and had an agent and went through the whole thing of doing meetings and castings, and very quickly I thought this is going to take away not only any desire to be creative or any opportunity to be creative but it's going to take my soul away really.

We [Kneehigh] believe in not only the collective but also the individual, and finding something new. You really have to do that when you work with people – when you're on the same journey of work as Kneehigh – for a long time.

Money wasn't a consideration, freedom was. So being rather po-faced then, the early days of Kneehigh, a maverick theatre company, gave you an enormous freedom. You were away from the big institutions and the big cities and the funding bodies and you were making work because you needed to make it and you wanted to get your hands dirty and you wanted to work really hard – the opposite of waiting for a phone to ring and hoping that you're going to get that advert and that it's going to solve your financial state. So those were the beginnings really and there were any number of theatre companies that were like that back then.

Certainly the roots of Kneehigh are to do with people belonging to something, that is, company spirit. It hasn't got a manifesto but if it did it would have words in it like play, anarchy, generosity, bravery, ambition ... And I think those words generosity and bravery are fairly key, because I think a lot of people are fearful – will I get that job, will I get the press?

There was a desire to tell the story, to entertain in the full extent, to make people laugh, and to engage people – that's the fundamental reason why we do theatre: to engage people.

The thing that you hear us say a lot is, you don't know, you don't know, but that's not necessarily a problem, hold your nerve, hold your nerve and something will come in, something will come in.

The barns are great as well because there's no mobile-phone signal, you can't pop out for a cappuccino, you have to learn to light the fire or you get cold, you have to cook or you'd be hungry. So all those practical things build a team and a spirit which you can then use in some way.

I quite often talk about what we do as the Church of Lost Causes. There is a communion that happens onstage. People are hungry for something different, that isn't act one, scene one, scene three, and isn't basically bloody boring.

David Ajala

We were taken to see *Aladdin*. And I thought wow. It was incredible because I believed in all that they were doing, and I believed that they were in this world and Aladdin existed. They called a few kids out of the audience to involve themselves with this act that they were doing. I remember just putting my hand up because I so wanted to be part of that world and I was like, please choose me, I want to be in that magical world.

That was my first experience in the theatre and then when I was in secondary school, I took it up as a GCSE, and at the same time I was in the Anna Scher Theatre, doing after-school lessons. And that's how it started. So I'm from a theatre background, even though I've done TV and stuff, but I think there's something magical and fresh and spontaneous about watching a theatrical performance and being able to affect it.

I love being able to communicate with people and to affect people's spirit, to make them laugh, to make them cry as well, I suppose, and it's a good release. Even as a businessman, you're selling a product, you have to be passionate about this product and you think that this product is good, not only is it good for yourself but it's good for the other person. It's that whole thing of expressing yourself and sharing yourself.

I think it's being able to be someone else and forget about yourself. I find that it's such a release to be able to go onstage and play a different character and leave David in the dressing room or whatever. It's so refreshing and it allows you to breathe. I think it works in a spiritual way.

What do I do? First, I read the script. I read the whole story. I try not to spend too long on my lines at all. I just whizz through it and I just . . . because the first time I read it, that's the first time I'm going to be able to enjoy it as an audience, and after that moment, it's all work, work, work. So I just skim through my lines, I skim . . . I read more through everyone's lines and then, after reading, I get the gist of the story. Then I look back at it and I see what my character says, what he does, what people say about him, and then I just keep reading it. I don't intentionally try to learn my lines.

I think you can do as much work as you want to or as little work as you want to, but I think the main thing is, you have to be prepared that whatever you've planned, or not planned, will be changed. It has the potential to be changed. So if you're willing to be able to be free and flexible, then you can do as much work as you want, and hopefully it'll pay off when you're rehearsing. I think it's just equipping yourself with many different ideas and ways of approaching the character, so when you're in a rehearsal process, you're able to disregard some or keep some. And it's so refreshing to be able to throw away things that you thought may have worked but don't. And it's good not to be attached to ideas as well, you need to be able to throw them away – the ones that don't work, and try not to over-cram your work.

I would say you have to know the reason why you want to be an actor. If you want to be an actor because you see how much some actors get paid in the Hollywood movies, then you've kind of skipped. I think it's important you know the work ethic it requires and you need to understand what you need to bring to the table as an actor. I think you have to go to a stage school or somewhere where you can become comfortable with your ability as an actor, because you yourself are the product, and you need to be comfortable with that, and you need to understand how your product works before even thinking about working on this or that.

This is the craft that you're studying, and this field of work and this subject of acting has gone on years before our time, so I think it's healthy to look into how acting was in the 1900s, how it was pre-1900s, research acting in different countries as well because it's not just the UK or America that does acting, it's all over.

I think as well as seeing great, fantastic productions, it's also good to see bad productions because you need to know what's good and what's bad, what works and what doesn't work. I think it's important that you're able to allow yourself to fail, especially in the rehearsal process. You need to be able to laugh at yourself, you need to be able to allow yourself to just be . . . not secret. You need to allow yourself to fail and to accept defeat, knowing that you'll be strong enough to overcome that in the near future.

CHAPTER 5

Production management

The production department is one of the busiest in a working theatre; as it launches one production on to the stage it's begun working on the next and it falls to the production manager and his or her team to organise and coordinate this process, calling on the skills of stage management, carpenters, electricians, scenic artists, sound and lighting.

Jobs in stage management

Production manager
Most often found in building-based theatre companies, production managers oversee all the technical departments and supervise the finances and scheduling of productions, ensuring that set, costume, lighting and sound are delivered on time and on budget.

Production managers function as the chief liaison between the different technical departments. They are not involved in the day-to-day running of one show, but supervise progress on entire seasons or repertoires.

Stage manager
The stage manager heads up the stage-management department and reports directly to the production manager. In commercial theatre the stage manager is usually called the company stage manager, and at touring theatres the on-site stage manager is referred to as the resident stage manager to differentiate between them and the stage manager of the visiting company.

In producing theatre companies the stage manager, usually supported by a team of deputies and assistants, is responsible for running the backstage operation of a production, supervising rehearsals, preparing the props and organising the day-to-day schedule. The job is complex and pressurised but requires a considerable amount of calm and stamina to carry it out effectively.

Deputy stage manager (DSM)

The DSM runs the rehearsals on a day-to-day basis, setting up the rehearsal room, looking after the director and cast, and making notes of all the decisions made during rehearsals in the prompt book. During the performance, the DSM prompts the actors and cues the technical crew.

Assistant stage manager (ASM)

Usually the most junior of the stage-management team, the ASM can be called on to do many things, from making or buying props to running errands or helping out in the rehearsal room. During the performance, the ASM will usually help out with set changes backstage.

Production process

Pre-production

One of the first jobs for the stage manager is to supervise auditions, both in terms of organising a place to hold them, making sure the location is prepared with the right tables and chairs etc., and arranging tea, coffee and refreshments. On the day, the stage manager deals with actors as they arrive at the audition and ensures that they have all their correct contact details before they leave. In addition, the pre-production period is taken up with planning the forthcoming rehearsals, from the arrangement of the rehearsal rooms to company liaison, ensuring that everyone in the cast and crew have copies of the script and that the stage-management team has a complete list of contact details for those involved.

The stage-management team will also source key props and furniture to use during the rehearsal period. These are not the ones that will be used in performance, but need to be a reasonable representation of the sort of props and furniture that will be. They will also provide practice skirts and jackets, if the play is a period piece, so that actors get used to the restrictions these items will impose on their performances.

Marking out

It is neither cost-effective nor time-efficient to build a replica of the set in the rehearsal room, so the stage-management team uses the designer's floor plan to mark out the set on the floor of the room, using different-coloured tape. Rehearsal rooms are typically the same size or larger than the stage space, so the whole stage area is marked out, with all the exits/entrances and significant aspects of the set, such as steps etc., clearly identified.

First rehearsal

This is a busy day for the stage-management team. It is their job to meet each member of the cast and creative team as they arrive and show them to the rehearsal room. The room is prepared with a circle or semicircle of chairs, plus a table on which the model box is placed. There must also be a plug point or extension cable nearby for the lighting designer, and increasingly a laptop computer, or the facility to link a laptop computer to a projector and screen, as more and more designers prepare their ideas digitally.

Once the director and designers have explained their approach to the production and the cast have read through the play, the stage manager will take the cast on a tour of the premises. If this is a building-based company, the tour will take in all the essential areas; if the production is being rehearsed in hired halls or rooms, it will be of the key facilities and the emergency exits and muster points. Finally, they will ensure that they have all the relevant information to pass on to the finance department, ensuring that the cast and additional crew are added to the payroll.

Rehearsals

The day-to-day routine of rehearsals usually begins with a stage-management meeting to discuss the agenda for the day. The DSM will run the rehearsal, prepare the rehearsal room and keep notes in the prompt book. The stage manager and the ASMs who are not in the rehearsal room with the DSM will be sourcing and making props, visiting props hire companies and generally making all the preparations for the production itself.

In rehearsals, the DSM watches the play, making lists of the props, furniture and effects that are decided upon. They note down the blocking of each scene – all the moves made by the actor – so that actors and director can refer to them if they need reminding at the next rehearsal. Blocking often needs to be notated quickly as performers won't stop to let the DSM catch up. The notes should be made in pencil as moves frequently change during the rehearsal period.

At the end of the day's rehearsal, the DSM meets with the director to confirm the scenes to be rehearsed the following day, before compiling the call sheet and posting it on the production noticeboard. The DSM also compiles the rehearsal note, listing any decisions and changes made during the day. The note is circulated to the whole technical crew as standard practice and in some companies will be circulated to all staff, so that they can remain informed of production progress. Towards the end of rehearsals, the actors reach 'book down', after which they may not use their script during the rehearsal session so the DSM acts as prompt where needed.

In addition to the daily stage-management meetings, once a week there will be a production meeting at which all the heads of technical departments discuss progress and ask any questions that have arisen. The stage manager keeps notes of these meetings and circulates them to those who attended as well as to all key personnel. Where a designer is unable to attend the meeting, the stage manager must ensure that they receive a copy of the notes as soon as possible.

As rehearsals draw to a close and the production heads towards technical week, the stage-management team must now prepare to supervise the technical week. After opening night, it is the stage management who are in charge of the production, and this is the point at which the team gear up for this responsibility. Where rehearsals have taken place in rooms away from the theatre venue, the stage management will arrange the transport of any furniture and props back into the theatre. Those that are to be used for the show will go to the wing space, while the rest will either be returned to the place or source they came from or, where surplus to requirement, thrown away. All markings are removed from the rehearsal floor and the room is left clean and tidy ready for the next set of rehearsals to commence.

Where props are being hired, this is when they will be collected and kept backstage ready to be moved into the theatre.

Prompt book

The prompt book is the production's bible. It is a record of all the entrances, exits, moves, props and cues established in rehearsal and it's what the DSM will use to cue the show throughout the run. Each stage manager will have their own unique style for marking up the book, but there are basic guidelines to be followed.

Most approaches require two copies of the script, separated into single pages. Using two pieces of plain hole-punched A4 paper, laid side by side, punched holes in the centre, the first page is stuck on to the right-hand piece of paper, towards its right-hand edge. This arrangement allows for notes to be made on the adjoining left-hand sheet of paper, as well as surrounding the text on the right-hand page. Two copies of the script are required, because in sticking down page one, the reverse of the page – page two – is obscured. Some stage managers divide the left-hand page into three columns, with the central column headed 'LX and SFX', the right-hand column headed 'Moves, Calls, Exits and Entrances', and the left-hand column headed 'Props and Scene Changes'. Once complete, the pages are placed in an A4 ring binder and each scene or unit is separated using file dividers.

When using a typed manuscript, usually for productions of new work, the stage manager won't need to use additional pages, using the blank page opposite the text for their notes instead. The prompt book is generally A4 in size and made up in a sturdy folder with a waterproof cover. Some stage managers also place individual pages inside protective plastic wallets, rather than risk a spilt cup of coffee or water ruining the work of three weeks of rehearsal!

Properties

Properties, or props, are all the small, non-permanent, movable items on set that are used by the actors during the performance. It is the stage management team's responsibility to source all the props required for the show and they do this by making, hiring, buying or borrowing them. Hired props usually come from companies who specialise in making and storing a huge range of props, from dinner services and dining-room chairs, to cigarette cases, handbags and standard lamps. They are particularly useful when attempting to prop a period production, as many hire companies keep complete sets of period items. For contemporary productions, it is often possible to buy or borrow most props, and, where the occasion demands, stage management will also make props, using lightweight materials and paint effects.

Firearms, swords and other weapons

A great many plays, particularly historical ones, feature weapons of some kind, and there are strict regulations regarding the handling and storage of such items. In the theatre, actors work with imitation weaponry, but these imitations often look very realistic. They must be handled responsibly and, when not in use, stored securely in a locked cabinet to guard against theft. The use of some types of weapon requires a licence from the local police and it is always a good idea to notify the police if the production intends to use weapons, of any kind. Blank ammunition should be supervised at all times and kept by the DSM during the performance and returned to secure storage immediately after it.

Get-in and fit-up

In most producing and touring theatres, the get-in and fit-up of a new production follows immediately on from the strike and get-out of the previous show, so the stage management will ensure that the stage area is cleared of all the previous set and props, swept clean and made ready for the installation of the new set. The production manager supervises the fit-up as a whole, while the stage-management team carry out their own preparations as well as liaising between the various technical departments and the production manager.

The stage-management team prepare their props tables and transfer everything from storage into the backstage area. The prompt book is finalised and the DSM writes up all the cue sheets, setting lists, scene-change plots, quick-change lists before passing them to the relevant personnel.

The production manager and stage-management team are responsible for the health and safety of all the cast and crew throughout the production. This not only means that they must ensure that staff carry out the fit-up using proper safety equipment, but that everyone is briefed on emergency procedures and that all fire extinguishers and safety equipment has been checked prior to commencement. Once the set is in and secure, the stage-management team assist the designer in dressing the set and position the movable items such as furniture.

Get-ins and fit-ups usually take place after one show closes on a Saturday night, and before the technical week begins on the Monday morning. Stage management and technical crew will work through the night and on into Sunday in order to get the stage ready for Monday morning's technical rehearsals. It is the production manager and stage manager's job to ensure that everyone working takes regular breaks. Many of these breaks are regulated by the unions who represent the backstage technical crew. The fit-up can be long and arduous, but is also a time of great energy and anticipation as the work of all the diverse departments comes together for the first time. Good stage management will ensure that this is a positive experience rather than a chore.

Lighting focus and plot
In this session the lighting designer, the director, the DSM and the lighting technician will go through each lighting state, checking the effect, confirming the cue and synchronising their timing of it. ASMs will assist the session, by walking through the scene from cue to cue so that those sitting in the auditorium can see the effect the lighting has.

Sound cueing
Sometimes combined with the lighting focus session, the sound session allows the sound designer and operator to run through all their cues and confirm them with the DSM. Today the majority of sound effects are recorded and played digitally, although in some productions recorded sound effects must be coordinated with live music and live sound effects.

Costume parade
This session often takes place immediately before the first dress rehearsal and resembles a fashion show, in that each actor appears

before the director, costume designer and wardrobe supervisor in each of the costumes that they will wear during the performance. Stage management must coordinate the running of this session, ensuring that actors change from one costume to the next in timely fashion, and take notes of changes as a backup to the designer's and wardrobe supervisor's notes.

Prompt corner

Before the technical rehearsal the DSM will prepare the prompt corner for the production. In most theatres this is a desk set in the wing space left or right and close to the front of the stage, giving the DSM a clear view of the set. In some theatres where this is not possible, CCTV is used to relay the action to a monitor used by the DSM backstage. The prompt corner will be the place from which the intercom and backstage communication and cueing systems are operated, and will also be where the production's prompt book is kept.

Each DSM prepares their prompt corner in a particular fashion. It is important to remember that it is the hub of the production, and no one should touch or move anything from the prompt corner without the DSM's knowledge or say-so. Scrabbling around for the prompt book five minutes before curtain-up because someone has moved it without warning does not make for a calm start to a show.

Backstage communications systems

Communication backstage is facilitated by the use of specialist intercom systems made up of several elements. The first uses pickup microphones over the stage to transfer the action onstage to a speaker system in the dressing rooms and actors' waiting areas. Known as the backstage relay, this allows those outside of the actual stage space to keep track of the play's progress. Another element of the system is an intercom connected to speakers in the front-of-house and foyer areas, which enables the DSM to make public announcements to the audience before curtain-up and during the interval. The last element of the comms system is specifically used by technical staff to cue effects and changes during the show. It is usually made up of three parts: a headset with microphone, a switching system and a set of red and green cue lights. Today these systems can be analogue cable-based systems requiring technical crew to wear a belt pack connected to a comms point somewhere in the backstage area, or digital remote systems that allow personnel to roam the backstage space without being inhibited by cables. The technical crew use the microphones to give verbal cues, while the cue lights are switched to red for 'Stand by' and then green for 'Go'. The DSM always gives a warning 'stand by' cue first before issuing a 'go' cue because technical staff are often doing several jobs at once. The 'stand by' cue serves to draw their attention to the fact that they have a cue coming up. The standard protocol for issuing cues is as follows:

DSM: Stand by, LX [lighting]. Cues ten and eleven. (A red light is given.)

LX operator: Standing by. (The LX operator flashes the red light to give a visual indication they have received the warning.)

DSM: LX, cue ten and eleven, go. (The green light is given.)

at which point the cue is executed.

Technical rehearsal

The purpose of the technical rehearsal is to put all elements of the production together for the first time. The backstage team can rehearse their participation, while the actors acclimatise themselves to the stage, set and costumes.

The production manager sits in the auditorium with the director and other members of the creative team, and it is their job to stop the rehearsal if asked by one of these people. Meanwhile, the stage manager is backstage on headphones and will stop the rehearsal at the request of one of the backstage technical staff, or when something goes wrong. In this instance, the stage manager appears onstage to brief the creative team on the problem, gives an estimate of how long a delay there will be and then supervises the resolution of the problem. The stage manager remains onstage while this happens, waiting for the clearance by the DSM to say that everyone is ready to continue. The stage manager then announces the point in the play at which the rehearsal will recommence and then steps back into the wings.

The DSM remains 'on the book' throughout, practising cues and altering them where necessary.

The technical rehearsal is the absolute and final point at which changes should be made.

Dress rehearsals

As with every other department, the dress rehearsals should be run as if actual performances. Stage management sets the stage ready for the beginning of the play, checks the props tables and runs through the cues. ASMs will check each actor has arrived and has collected any personal props they need to carry with them. They will liaise with wardrobe to supervise the positioning of costumes or quick changes and generally ensure that everything is prepared for the performance. Thirty-five minutes prior to curtain-up the DSM will begin the backstage calls.

So for an effective stage-management team, apart from the missing audience, this is a performance and the aim is that everything goes smoothly. Although theatre tradition insists that a bad dress rehearsal makes for a good opening night, few stage managers set out to intentionally make it so.

Previews

With complex and technically difficult productions, previews can often become additional dress rehearsals, and on occasions might have to be cancelled altogether. For the smooth-running show, they offer an opportunity to hone the efficiency of the production and prepare for the opening night, as well as to change or alter anything that isn't working.

Opening night

The key ingredient of the opening night among the cast is nerves and this is where a well-established schedule and the calm assurance of a relaxed stage-management team can be highly effective – if stage management are panicked and flustered, this energy will transfer itself to the cast. Difficulties and delays should be handled quickly, but quietly, and the cast informed of problems only where it is likely that these will directly affect them.

Running the show should now be a well-practised routine, and once the stage is set and cleared the DSM can cue the house manager to let in the audience. When everyone is seated the show can begin.

The run

The stage-management team are now in charge of the production. Each day they will carry out their pre-show checks, fixing, replacing or renewing items where necessary. At the end of each performance the DSM will compile a show report which is circulated to each of the company's departments. This report will include anything of note that happened during the performance, an indication of audience numbers and which sections of the play they seemed particularly to appreciate, as well as the show's running time. It will also note down any item of set, costume, props, lighting or sound that needs attention.

Strike and get-out

After the final performance, the production manager and stage-management team supervise the strike of the set. In the first instance, all props and portable furniture are removed to the on-site store, then the technical crew begin dismantling the set. Some items will be stored, some will be recycled and others will be scrapped, usually placed in a large skip outside the scene-dock doors. Once the stage is clear of set, the lighting crew can de-rig the lights, and the whole space is swept clean. During the following week, props, furniture and set items will be returned to the theatre's permanent storage space, or sent back to the companies they were hired from.

Finding out more

Aveline, Joe, *Production Management*, Entertainment Technology Press, 2002

Bond, Daniel, *Stage Management – A Gentle Art*, A & C Black, 1991

Davies, Gill, *The Complete Stage Planning Kit*, A & C Black, 2003

Davies, Gill, *Stage Source Book: Props*, A & C Black, 2004

Dean, Peter, *Production Management: Making Shows Happen: A Practical Guide*, Crowood, 2002

Hoggett, Chris, *Stage Crafts*, 2nd edn, A & C Black, 2001

Maccoy, Peter, *Essentials of Stage Management*, A & C Black, 2004

Pallin, Gail, *Stage Management: The Essential Handbook*, Nick Hern Books, 2003

CHAPTER 6

The set designer

Today, theatre design encompasses the disciplines of set, costume, make-up, lighting and sound. A set designer's task is to produce an artificial space that serves the needs of the play and the performers who act within it. However, a good design does much more than this; it enhances a production, and its imaginative use of space, tone, colour and style give the design a unique creativity that, while not overpowering the other elements of the production, adds another level to the interpretation of the text. Good design can heighten the drama of the text and present it to an audience in a way which complements and underlines the action, sense of mood and atmosphere. In essence, good design is fundamental to creating the world of the play.

The set design is the first thing the audience encounters when they enter the auditorium and it has several tasks to achieve before the play has even begun. It locates the play geographically in a way the audience can understand, whether that is a suburban drawing room, or the desert plains of Nevada. It also provides an indication of style – a detailed box-set drawing room, with three walls, curtains, carpet, three-piece suite, etc., would tend to suggest a realistic production, while a lack of walls, a free-standing window and stylised furniture might suggest a minimalist or symbolist version. Design can also suggest more abstract ideas, such as class and belief – a room dominated by Christian symbols tells us something of the people who use it, as does whether the room is tidy or cluttered, well furnished or spartan, richly decorated or shabby. Design is not an arbitrary collection of walls and furniture.

Some of the world's greatest artists and architects – from Christopher Wren and Inigo Jones to Picasso, Miró and Hockney – have designed sets for theatre.

Production process

Pre-production
Set designers initially read the script and analyse it visually. The designer needs to discover the mood of the play, whether there are specific historical or geographical elements, what the play's strong

and continuous themes are, and what images these might suggest. She or he must identify the key scenes in terms of dramatic action and explore where design can enhance or heighten this action.

The designer will then meet up with the director, who may have very specific ideas about how they want the set realised. They might have a definite colour scheme in mind, or a preliminary floor plan sketched out. Then again, a director's ideas may not be very clear. They might suggest images or abstract themes that they want to focus on and are looking for the design to amplify these elements. It is the designer's job to transform these ideas, often referred to as the design brief – though rarely a clear or formal document – using their skill, imagination, inspiration and technical knowledge, to create a visual image closest to what the director wants.

Research
Designers need a comprehensive understanding of historical period, social anthropology, art, architecture and fashion, to complement their technical ability in construction. During this period of the production, research might involve visiting museums and buildings of specific architectural relevance, trips to special collections and archives, or days in art galleries trying to soak up a sense of period or style. The designer will make sketch copies of elements of particular interest, from architectural detailing, the look, tone or colour composition of a great painting, to a specific texture or effect that they want to reproduce within their design.

From this will come a series of ideas and rough sketches, which they will take to the director to discuss. From this discussion the designer will have a clear idea of which elements of their concept fit and which will need to be discarded. Some designers will then make a final set of sketches to show to the director, while others will move straight on to the next stage.

Line and balance
For a design to be effective, balance must be achieved throughout the main planes and lines (surfaces and edges) of the set as well as in its textures and tones (materials and colours). A set is a three-dimensional, dynamic space that needs to mimic reality but allow the artificiality of the theatre, so it doesn't always follow that the true architecture of our buildings and spaces provide the ideal.

Set model
Most design briefs – the contract that lays out what is expected of the designer – require a 'model box', the term given to the scale version of the stage and set that is used to demonstrate various aspects of

the production to cast and crew. Made from card, foam board or balsa wood, the model box is made at a scale of 1:25cm, i.e. a scale where one centimetre on the model is equivalent to twenty-five centimetres onstage. This is a universally applied convention and allows the production team to use the model box to give them appropriate measurements for the actual stage. Whatever appears in the model box must be necessary to the production, which might seem obvious, but nothing should be left to chance – it is not enough to use some shop-bought doll's house furniture of inappropriate style, shape or scale simply for ease or convenience, because the production team will seek to re-create these items exactly to scale. Special techniques, textures or effects must be reproduced within the model box, often with the true scale example to accompany it.

Technical drawings
In addition to the set model, the designer must also supply a complete set of technical drawings. In the first instance, the designer will be given a detailed, annotated scale ground plan of the auditorium and stage area, and will use this as a template for their floor plans, showing each different set-up of the design. The ground plan is the layout view and, to accompany it, the designer will either make sketches and technical scale drawings of specific items or detailing they require.

First rehearsal
At the first rehearsal the designer shows the model box to the cast, the technical team and other members of the company that might be present, such as the marketing department. While some people, particularly on the technical team, will have seen the design before, for most it is their first introduction to the vision of the production. It's the designer's job to present the design, scene by scene, act by act, or development by development, explaining how the changes are made – whether by flying an element in or out, moving items hydraulically or manually, or simply by changing the configuration of elements that are already on the stage. The aim is to give everyone a sense of how the actual set will work. This is not just a technical presentation; a good designer sells the design to cast and crew, engaging them in the energy and creativity of it as well as the nuts-and-bolts functionality. Actors or crew who are not confident in the design and who do not understand it, at best will not maximise its potential and at worst may damage or mishandle it.

Rehearsals
Once the play goes into its rehearsal period, the role of the designer will vary depending on the type of company he or she is working

for. Building-based theatre companies and commercial production companies usually have their own construction workshops or contract this work out to scenic construction companies. The designer's model and plans will be handed over to the production manager, who will supervise the implementation, regularly updating the designer on progress.

Construction workshop

Most building-based companies have their own construction workshop, headed by a master carpenter, assisted by chippies (carpenters) and other technical staff. The workshops will build all the sets for the production, including rostra, trucks and flats. Stage carpenters are skilled at creating illusions. Solid walls are usually nothing more than several flats tied together and covered in a special paint effect, while a marble façade is polystyrene, cardboard tubing and another paint effect. The key to stage construction is that items are light, portable and can be easily put up and taken down.

Flats

One tool used for constructing sets is the scenic flat, a large rectangular wooden frame stretched with canvas, sized and then painted. Each flat can be braced and held in place with a stage weight, and several flats can be tied together to form walls of other structures.

Rostra and trucks

Rostra are rectangular wooden platforms of varying heights that are used to create different levels onstage. Many theatre companies have a basic stock of collapsible rostra, while others build rostra when and where a production demands it.

Trucks are rostra used to carry static scenery that needs to be moved on and offstage regularly, such as for reoccurring locations in a play. To facilitate their transport, manual trucks are placed on castors and manoeuvred into place by stagehands before brakes are applied. Some theatres make use of a hydraulic trucking system, powered by compressed air and controlled either manually by the stage manager or with computer software.

Scenic workshop

The scenic workshop is headed by the scenic artist – again with two or three assistants – and it is their job to carry out any painting work, either on the set or of large backdrops or cycloramas placed at the back of the stage.

To enable this, the scenic artist has a paint frame, a large metal framework, on to which a canvas the full size of the backstage wall can be stretched for painting. This frame is usually accessed by a special scaffold that can be raised and lowered and moved from side to side, or in some cases the frame is mechanised and can be dropped into or raised from a trench in the floor.

Working on such a scale is a unique skill and most scenic artists have trained in fine art as well as scenic art. They need to understand a full range of painting techniques and must be as familiar with the domestic paintbrush and the paint gun as they are with a set of fine-bristled artist's brushes. Like their construction workshop colleagues, scenic artists are also geniuses at disguise and can use paint effects to create perspective, depth or shadow, and give the illusion of three dimensions to a flat surface.

Technical week

It is stage management's job to supervise the get-in and fit-up of the set but most designers are on hand to oversee this process and deal with any difficulties that might arise. Once the set is installed and made secure, the designer will apply any necessary effects or add-ons that can be put in place only on the completed set – for example, an overall effect such a shading, discoloration or damp won't be added to individual flats for fear that, on assembling them, the effect is not uniform. Once any effects or techniques have been added and 'gone off', i.e. dried or sealed, the designer will dress the set with the help of the ASMs. Dressing is the art of adding appropriate decoration to the set to make it look like the real environment, whether that is our archetypal sitting room or a post-apocalyptic war zone!

For the designer this is an exhausting and anxious period. It is the culmination of all their planning and creativity. Throughout the technical and dress rehearsals, the designer will sit in the auditorium with the director and the other members of the creative team making notes on things that work, fail or need adapting. Sometimes ideas that the designer or director have had, when realised, don't work or are too distracting and the designer might have to scrap whole elements of the set at the last minute. Similarly, they might find themselves having to add or construct new elements thanks to changes in emphasis, theme or approach which have only evolved through recent rehearsal, and such is the nature of theatre. The key here is that the designer must remain flexible and open, as well as creative, right up to the opening night.

After opening night, the designer's work is usually complete. The exception to this is where company decides to take a static production on tour, in which case the designer may be commissioned either to convert their design for touring, or to carry out a complete redesign.

Designing the touring show
The most obvious difference between the design for a touring show and a static one is that at regular intervals the touring set must be deconstructed, packed, transported and reassembled in a different venue – sometimes for a different company. This calls for a design that is sturdy, lightweight and quick to assemble. What should not be assumed is that this means an easy or reduced design. Instead, the demands on the designer are greater, as they must find a way to create a concept for the show that meets all the above criteria but also demonstrates imagination and sets the right mood and atmosphere for the production.

Finding out more

Gillette, J. Michael, *Theatrical Design and Production*, 5th edn, McGraw-Hill, 2005

Goodwin, John, ed., *British Theatre Design: The Modern Age*, Weidenfeld & Nicolson, 1989

Hoggett, Chris, *Stage Crafts*, A & C Black, 1991

Holt, Michael, *Stage Design and Properties: A Phaidon Theatre Manual*, revised edn, Phaidon Press, 1993

Orton, Keith, *Model Making for the Stage*, Crowood Press, 2004

Pecktal, Lynn, *Designing and Drawing for the Theatre*, McGraw-Hill, 1995

Reid, Francis, *Designing for the Theatre*, A & C Black, 1996

Thorne, G., *Stage Design: A Practical Guide*, Crowood Press, 1999

CHAPTER 7

The costume designer

The role of costume in theatre is extraordinarily important, whether it be for a period production or the most contemporary of new plays, and theatrical costume-making is a highly specialised skill that draws together a talent for fashion and design, an understanding of period style and an ability to devise unique methods of achieving required looks. The clothes worn onstage by actors fulfil many different functions. The audience uses costume to tell them certain things – what period the play is set in, what the status of a character is – as well as conveying more subtle information about a character's personality – the well-dressed person who fusses about their appearance is not the same as the sloppy individual with stains on their shirt who looks a mess whatever clothes they wear.

Jobs in costume design

Costume designer

The costume designer is responsible for designing all the costumes worn by the actors during the performance. They must inevitably have a love of fashion and clothing, but unlike their fashion-industry colleagues, they will also have a sense of period cut, the eye of a fine artist in the way that costumes can be used as a creative statement or ideal, together with a thorough understanding of the way clothing functions as part of history, culture and society.

Wardrobe supervisor

The wardrobe supervisor is usually an experienced costumier with excellent organisational skills, an encyclopedic knowledge of fabrics, style and periods, as well as someone who understands the pressure of theatre deadlines. It is their job to liaise with the costume designer and their team to create, fit and finish each costume on time and on budget.

Wardrobe assistant

Cutters and stitchers will be trained and experienced in the creation of patterns from scratch, a well as the weave and hang of fabrics. They cut, pin and tack a design for fitting to the actor, and will then complete the garment, ensuring that it can endure many performances.

Wardrobe technician
The wardrobe department utilises a range of different techniques to create special period details and effects for theatrical costumes, and the department will employ or contract in freelance staff to carry out these specialised aspects of costuming, from millinery to corseting.

Underwear and corsetry specialist
The use of corsets, crinolines and other undergarments in the past often affected the look and line of an outfit, and in order to reproduce this look, it may be necessary to re-create the right type of underwear. A specialist in lingerie and underwear will be able to reconstruct the appropriate historical look using contemporary materials and adapted to the needs of the actor.

Dyeing and distressing specialist
Where a period colouring or effect is no longer available, technicians who are skilled in dyeing techniques might be required. Similarly, it may be necessary for a costume to appear old or tattered onstage. It's not possible to use an old garment, because it would not withstand the continued use required for a production run. Instead, a new garment is used and special techniques applied to give the appearance of age.

Dresser
The dresser is the theatre equivalent of a valet, dressing the actor in each of their costumes. Before the 1950s it was common practice for each leading actor to have their own personal dresser, who often travelled with them from show to show, getting to know the actor's likes and dislikes and eventually functioning more as a personal assistant than a dresser. In theatres today, this practice is rare. The majority of actors, especially in contemporary productions, will dress themselves, and even in period plays, most of the basic costume will be put on by the actor, with the dresser checking the costume over to ensure it is being worn correctly. Where actors have complicated costumes, wigs and hats it is customary to use a dresser, and when quick changes are made in the wing space, one or two dressers may be required. Dressing is not an occupation for the shy. Actors often make costume changes at speed and will not be demure or discreet about removing their clothes. The dresser must take any state of undress in their stride and get on with the job of getting the actor into their next outfit.

Production process

Pre-production

The costume designer will read the play several times, making notes on any ideas that occur to them, as well as information on character and stage directions that require specific costuming.

The designer will have an initial discussion with the director, from which they will get a sense of the director's interpretation and approach. At this point the costume designing will be a collection of ideas and rough notated sketches, but the designer will already know whether the costumes are to be realistic, abstract or interpretative. The realistic design aims to accurately reproduce the period or style that is indicated by the setting of the play – say, Elizabethan England or New Orleans at the turn of the twentieth century – whereas an abstract approach will isolate an idea or theme from the play and then express it non-naturalistically through the costume, often by choice of shape and colour. Interpretative design is based in reality, so that shape and cut might conform to period or style, but instead of accurate reproduction of all fabrics, cuts and colours, the designer may choose one tonal range for all the costumes, or a single type of fabric for one group of characters, with another type for the rest. These choices will be made in order to emphasise a theme of the play, usually in line with the director's interpretation.

The designer will visit museums and specialist costume collections for inspiration as well as gathering formal information on construction and fabric composition. Art galleries are also a great source of information, period portraiture containing an invaluable record of fashion and colour for both men and women. At the end of this process, the designer will finalise their plans by making up the costume sketches in time for the first production meeting.

First rehearsal

At the first rehearsal the costume designer will present the sketches to the assembled company and cast, explaining each costume and the motivation for the choices made. These sketches are final drawings that show the costume in detail and in colour. The sketch will be on a single sheet of paper, and there will be illustrations of any particular costume detailing, as well as small samples of the costume's fabric (known as swatches) attached. Some designers like to include a visual reference – a painting or illustration to help put the design into context. Some designers notate their sketches, indicating where specialist techniques will be required.

In addition to the costume presentation, the wardrobe supervisor must find time to carry out detailed measuring sessions with each actor. While the actors' basic measurements are usually supplied as part of their performance CVs, wardrobe will require the most up-to-date measurements, not just because an actor may have gained or lost weight, but because different types of costuming require different types of measurement. Costumes are made specifically to fit individual actors, and if a play has a long run and several casts, each new cast member will have their own versions of their character's costumes.

Rehearsals

In building-based theatre companies with their own wardrobe staff, a designer will not be on-site throughout rehearsals. Instead, they will attend the theatre for the regular production meetings and usually combine this visit with a catch-up meeting with the wardrobe supervisor. In addition, the costume designer will often accompany the wardrobe supervisor when they go to buy the costume fabrics, to eliminate the possibility of error in choice of fabric. Alternatively, the designer and the wardrobe supervisor may choose fabric from a sample book supplied by a specialist fabric wholesaler. Buying fabric this way can be very economical. The wardrobe supervisor can order it in any length, and do so on account, thus allowing the theatre to pay for the fabric in manageable stages. If the production is to use hired costumes, the designer will visit the costumiers with the supervisor or one of their assistants, to ensure that the costumes ordered for the production are the ones that arrive at the theatre for the start of technical week.

Once the fabrics arrive, they are washed, as many fabrics shrink on initial washing. If this is not done, the costume will be cut, stitched and fitted to the actor, only to shrink when it is laundered after the first night. The fabric is then pressed and passed to the cutters, who will make up a pattern according to the designer's sketch then cut, pin and tack all the pieces together ready for the actor's first fitting. In some cases where a costume is very complex or to be made from expensive fabric, wardrobe will first construct a toile, a mock-up of the costume made from toile cotton or muslin. The toile will be used in the first fitting, then adjusted and altered until designer and wardrobe are happy. Only then will the altered pieces be cut from the fabric and made up. This is to avoid both wastage and errors in construction, particularly where fabrics have weaves or patterns that affect how they hang or are made. Fittings must be arranged around the actors' rehearsal commitments, and there will usually be at least two fittings before the costume is finalised. The wardrobe supervisor coordinates with the production's DSM on a daily basis to determine which actors are available and which are not, and some deft organisational skills are required, as availability shifts on an hour-by-hour basis.

As the production approaches technical week, the costumes are completed and pressed, and placed on hangers that carry the actor's name and the character they play, together with the scene the costume is worn for. The actor's name is also sewn into the back of the costume, not because the actor is forgetful, but because several waistcoats of the same colour and fabric may look the same but, as we have seen, each is in fact individually sized. The name tape allows the actor to find their costume at speed.

Get-in and fit-up
During the get-in and fit-up, the wardrobe team will be making ready the actors' dressing rooms and placing the actors' costumes in wearing order on a temporary rail. Each costume will be accompanied where necessary with the relevant accessories – shoes, hats, wigs. The wardrobe assistants will also set up the quick-change area in the wing space, where possible, or as close as possible to the stage, where wing space is unavailable. The quick-change area needs a lighting source that will allow the dressers to carry out their job, but which will not spill out on to the stage. If an exit or entrance depends on the completion of a quick change, this will also need to be integrated into the DSM's communication system so that the DSM can give red 'warn' and green 'go' lights to the dressers.

Technical week
The actors' first experience of their costumes will be as part of the technical rehearsals and while they are not required to act at full intensity during these rehearsals, it does provide the costume designer, the wardrobe supervisor and the actors a chance to see how the costumes work, separately and together. The designer will sit in the auditorium and make notes on anything that needs changing or altering, while the actors will draw attention to any aspect of the costume that seriously impedes their performance. The wardrobe assistants, now functioning mostly as dressers or quick-change dressers, have the opportunity to implement their routine and establish whether the quick changes work. Where they don't, an additional dresser may be required or, in the most extreme cases, a costume will need to be rethought in order for it to be realised in the time available.

Dress rehearsals
The dress rehearsal is the first opportunity for the costume designer and the wardrobe team to see the costume in action. It will demonstrate how hardy a costume is, and how much wear and tear it can expect during the run of the production. In some cases costumes will be damaged and require repair, while in others it will become

clear that the costume doesn't work in some respect. Rapid repair or reassessment is required to ensure that a final costume is arrived at in time for opening night, and it is not unheard of for an actor to be seen in one costume at the first preview and a totally different one by the opening night!

The run
From the dress rehearsal onwards the wardrobe department works to a regular daily schedule, laundering and checking costumes and carrying out running repairs. Costumes must be laundered frequently – adrenalin causes actors to perspire more than they usually would, as does the intense heat produced by stage lighting, and three hours onstage can be the equivalent of a week's ordinary wear. Not all costumes can be easily laundered, and in some cases wardrobe will make two of an item to enable one to be worn while the other is being washed.

Strike and get-out – costume storage
On the last night of the play's run, the costumes will be returned to wardrobe and laundered for the final time. Where a costume has been hired, it will be returned to the costumier, and where the costume has been made specially, it will either be added to the costume store, or be broken down to be reused in another context. Some theatres make use of their costume store, hiring out costumes for fancy-dress parties or local amateur dramatic productions. However, maintenance and storage costs can be expensive and many theatres will either sell their costumes to commercial costumiers or dispose of them.

Finding out more

Bicat, Tina, *The Handbook of Stage Costume*, Crowood Press, 2006
Bicat, Tina, *Making Stage Costumes – A Practical Guide*, Crowood Press, 2001
Bicat, Tina, *Period Costume for the Stage*, Crowood Press, 2003
Holt, Michael, *Costume & Make Up*, Schirmer Books, 1991
Ingham, Rosemary, and Covey, Liz, *Costume Designer's Handbook*, Heinemann, 1992
Peacock, John, *The Story of Costume*, Thames & Hudson, 2006

CHAPTER 8

The lighting designer

The importance of lighting and sound in the theatre increases exponentially as theatre technology itself advances, and designers seek to push the boundaries of what can be achieved within the artificial theatre environment. Although experiments with lighting began in Renaissance Italy, it was not until the introduction of gaslight in the 1800s that any really controllable effects could be achieved. The move to electricity improved safety and gradually improved control still further, but it was the development of the rock-music industry that really boosted stage lighting and sound. Technology developed to allow bands to fill huge sporting arenas for their concerts; more sophisticated lanterns, mixing desks, lighting desks and all manner of sound and amplification equipment could be adapted for use on the domestic stage, an innovatory relationship that continues today.

Good lighting and sound do more than simply enhance a play, they add to the overall artistic vision. Good sound helps build mood and atmosphere, while good lighting adds to the effect of set, costumes and performance – in some instances, light itself is the design.

Jobs in lighting

Lighting designer
The lighting designer is usually a freelance independent artist, not employed permanently by a theatre company but hired on a production-by-production basis. Many lighting designers establish close working partnerships with a small group of directors at the start of their careers, and it is not uncommon for a director to bring several members of a creative team with him or her, when hired by a theatre.

The lighting designer's job is to create an artistic response in light to the text. They must take this creative response and translate it into the physical lighting plot, which indicates the type of light to be used, where it should be placed and whether it should be coloured. The skill of a lighting designer requires in-depth knowledge of technical equipment, as well as an understanding of how natural light functions and how these natural states can be reproduced or interpreted for the stage.

Chief electrician

The chief electrician is traditionally found in both producing and receiving building-based theatre companies, and supervises the theatre's lighting and electrical systems. They might be required to fix a light in one of the administration offices, or rewire the box office for a new computer system, and they must do this in addition to their responsibilities for the stage-lighting equipment.

The chief electrician manages the electrics department, schedules its day-to-day work, supervises stock and ordering of electrical equipment, and liaises with each lighting designer over the realisation of their design concept. Chief electricians may themselves have design experience, but even if they don't, they will be thoroughly conversant with all aspects of lighting design. While the chief will supervise the implementation of the design, it is the rest of the team that will be responsible for its practical realisation.

Deputy chief electrician

Where a company has both a chief and a deputy, the deputy will take on some of the chief's duties, often the day-to-day maintenance of equipment and processes such as PAT testing, whereby electrical items used by the company must be checked to see that they are safe before being used. It is often the deputy's job to maintain and programme the lighting board, installing plots and cues during a production's lighting session.

Assistant electrician

Where employed by a company, the assistant electrician is the most junior member of the team, and often newly qualified from a relevant stage technician's course. On a day-to-day basis, their jobs will include rigging, focusing and maintaining the lighting stock, and running the lighting board during performance.

Production process

Pre-production

The lighting designer establishes their lighting brief following discussions with the production's director and the rest of the design team. Because lighting is only one of a number of design elements, the lighting designer must liaise constantly with the other designers, so that there are no sudden surprises later on. The designer will read the play a number of times, making notes on required lighting states – the time of day, the geographical location of scenes as well as the time of year they take place. The designer will then add these elements to the discussions had with the director and their own ideas arising from reading the play to make an artistic interpretation of the play through light. If a scene is set outside, for example, there may be no indication of time of day or year for the scene, but because of the director's vision of the play and the lighting designer's creative interpretation, they may choose to set it at night in winter, using cold steel-blue lighting effects in order to highlight a theme of 'bitterness'. It is in this way that lighting is both a practical and creative art.

Once the lighting designer has seen the model box, and received their copy of the ground plan with the set marked on it, they will 'grid up' the space into squares.

Principles of lighting

In the artificial environment of the theatre, lighting is often seeking to reproduce effects found in the natural world. The designer must ensure that the actors are lit, that lighting complements the action and mood of the scene, and that it enhances the costumes and set.

To reproduce natural light, as though an actor were being lit by the sun, the designer will use three lights: two front lights, positioned at 45 degrees above and to the side of the actor, and one backlight, positioned behind the actor at 45 degrees to them. This angle most accurately represents the way sunlight strikes the earth.

How a designer utilises this basic principle will depend on the type of show being staged and where it is set. If the play takes place in one fixed location, it is likely that the designer will use their grid system to set up a general cover in a warm colour and a cold colour, to offer 'day' and 'night', before adding any specials – that is light that will be used for specific scenes, effects or moments of the play. If, however, the play has multiple locations, requiring a number of times of day and climate, a designer will have to be more creative in how they utilise the light, drawing on a number of other lighting possibilities.

First rehearsal

At the first rehearsal, the lighting designer will present their ideas to the assembled company and cast after the set designer has presented the overall design. The lighting designer may do this using the model box or a series of sketches based on the model box, and some may use graphics software on a laptop computer. After their presentation, the lighting designer will answer any questions raised by the cast, before meeting separately with the production team to discuss the design in detail, including the hire of any specialist equipment. The lighting designer will also hand over their technical drawings of the lighting plot to the chief electrician.

Rehearsals

During the rehearsal period the designer will attend the regular production meetings, and be kept up to date in between by the chief electrician. Each day the chief will receive a copy of the previous day's rehearsal notes and this will tell them if any effects or scenes have been changed in such a manner as to affect the lighting. Sometimes there will be specific lighting notes, asking questions or requesting a specific effect not already contained within the design. The chief will often deal with questions raised, but additional requirements must be checked with the designer.

At this point the electrics team will also begin to prepare the lanterns that will be used for the production. Most building-based theatre companies will have a large lighting stock, whereas touring theatre companies will keep a smaller stock, hire their lanterns or just make use of the lights installed at the venue that they're visiting. This preparation will include cleaning and maintaining the lanterns and carrying out any necessary repairs. Many of the lanterns may already be in use on the play that's currently running in the theatre, while some lanterns, especially ones that execute special effects, may have to be hired specifically for the production. The teams will also ensure that any gels required to colour the lanterns have been prepared, and gobos (screens used in front of a light to project a shape) ordered or retrieved from stock.

Get-in and fit-up

Once the stage has been cleared of the previous production it is usual for the lighting to be rigged first, followed by the installation of the set. Many modern theatres have lighting grids that are suspended above the stage on a hydraulic or motorised mechanism that allows the entire rig to be lowered to the stage floor, where the lanterns can be fixed to it before being raised back into the flies. Otherwise, the rigging will be carried out using ladders and a tallescope, a mobile scaffold structure that allows riggers to access the grid from an elevated cubicle. It is for this reason that the rigging of lights takes place before the construction of set, as once the set is in place, it might be difficult to reach certain lighting positions.

Sometimes the lighting designer leads the rigging session, while on other occasions it will be the chief electrician who's in charge, using the lighting designer's technical drawings. The lights are not focused at this point, but any gels or gobos required will be added. Once the lights are in place, they will be checked to ensure they're secure and have safety chains fitted before the all-clear is given for the set team to move in.

Basic stage lantern

The lantern itself is made up of a bulb and bulb holder, a reflector, a lens and the steel casing that encloses it. The bulbs used in stage lighting are much more powerful than those used in domestic houses, giving off anything up to 2,000 watts. Consequently, they produce a considerable amount of heat and must be handled with great care when in use. Touching the glass of these bulbs can significantly reduce their life, as the oils contained in the skin leave a residue, which when heated can cause the glass to explode. For this reason new bulbs are installed using 'clean' gloves.

Each lantern is cuboid or rectangular in shape and has a short power cable at one end connected to a 6 or 15-amp plug. Across the same end of the lantern, there is a free-standing U-shaped yoke or clamp fitted to each of the longer sides of the lantern by a screw. This screw can be loosened and fastened to allow the lantern to tilt at varying angles. Fitted to the centre of the yoke is a G clamp, which fits on to the lighting bar and is secured by tightening a screw. Additional safety is provided by a steel chain or wire that is secured about the yoke and the lighting bar.

There are five classes of light, or lantern, used in professional theatre, providing two categories of lighting effect: a generalised soft light or a specific sharp-edged beam.

Floodlights

Floods give an even spread of light across a wide area of the stage. The beam produced is soft-edged and there is no lens present in this type of lantern. The beam cannot be focused or directed and in general these lights are used to provide a wash of light, usually across a cyclorama or backdrop. Floodlights come in single lantern units or in battens – pre-constructed groups of four or six floodlights that can be suspended from the rig, or placed on the floor of the stage.

Parcan

The parcan gives a soft-edged, but powerful elliptical beam of light that can be angled to cover specific areas of the stage. The lantern is made up of a lamp, reflector and lens in a fixed, unmoving unit somewhat like a car headlamp, and the effect produced is not subtle. The size of this lantern's beam cannot be altered, but very narrow beam, narrow beam, medium flood and wide flood varieties of parcan are available, as are 'birdies', a smaller version of the parcan better suited to lighting smaller spaces.

Fresnel

The fresnel throws a soft-edged beam of light and is composed of a lamp, a reflector and a graduated lens. The angle of the beam can be varied by moving the lamp closer to or further away from the reflector. Moving the lamp closer to the reflector produces an intense spot of light, whereas moving the lamp away from the reflector produces a wide wash of colour. Fresnels are often used with 'barn doors', hinged metal flaps that surround the light and can be swung inwards or outwards on all four sides to counteract spill and allow the beam to be shaped.

Pebble convex spotlight

The pebble convex, or PC spotlight, is a modern variety of fresnel spotlight that offers more control over the beam of light the lantern produces. It has greater range than the fresnel, but its light is harder to blend into general washes with other lanterns. The key difference between the fresnel and the PC is in the type of lens used. The prism convex lens is thinner than that used in the fresnel and is not grooved, but frosted. It is one of the chief lanterns used in lighting acting areas.

Profile spotlight

The profile spotlight produces a hard-edged beam of light that can be varied according to the position of one or more lenses contained inside the lantern casing. Unlike the flood, the fresnel or the parcan, the profile spotlight's lamp is fixed in front of the reflector, while its lenses moves to alter the size and sharpness of the beam of light. A profile spot can also be altered using an iris, dropped into the lantern's gate, an opening that occurs after the lamp but before the lenses. This gate can also be used for gobos, while gels are attached in a gel frame to the front. Barn doors are not necessary with this type of lantern. A follow spot is a specialised version of this type of lantern, attached to a base that allows the lantern to be panned and tilted freely. It requires its own operator and produces a hard-edged beam of light that 'follows' a performer about the stage.

Motorised Vari-Lites

This is the most contemporary type of lighting available today, and was developed initially for lighting rock concerts. These lanterns are extremely expensive and, in terms of their use in theatre, still in their early stages of development. For this reason very few companies buy Vari-Lites, preferring to hire them should the need arise. However, there is little doubt that these are the future of stage lighting.

The Vari-Lite is available in both profile and fresnel version and its significant innovation is that it can change its shape, direction, angle, colour and gobo throughout the performance. It does this in one of two ways. The first uses a system of motorised mirrors, which means that the light remains static, but by moving a combination of mirrors the direction, angle and shape of the light is altered. The colour of the lantern is altered using another motor, which rotates a gel disc or series of discs to achieve the right colour combination. The second method uses motors to control the yoke of the lantern, allowing it to be panned and tilted in any direction, while an internal motor alters the shape, intensity and colour of the beam.

There are significant drawbacks to the motorised systems, however – not least the noise level produced by the motors. Because these lighting systems were developed for the music industry, where noise levels are not an issue, in the quieter environment of the theatre, they can often be distracting. Furthermore, there is not, as yet, enough subtlety in the lighting that these lanterns produce, although this is a disadvantage that is rapidly being decreased as the systems advance. As is the need for a separate lighting desk simply to control the Vari-Lites in use, largely due to the complexity of the operations being controlled. But more advanced software programs, coupled with the general advance of lighting desks, means that at the high end of theatre use, fixed and Vari-Lites can now be operated through the same desk.

Gels
So-called because they were initially made of coloured gelatine, today's stage gels are made of plastic film. Gels come in large rolls and are specifically cut to fit a gel holder, a metal frame which slots on the front of the lantern. Gels alter the colour of the beam of light to create mood, atmosphere or environment. For example, the beam of light a lamp produces is not a replica of natural light, so for this a 'straw'-coloured yellow gel is added to create the natural light, while pale blue gels are often used to create moonlight.

Gobos
These are metal plates, which have patterns cut out of them, rather like stencils. They are placed in front of the lamp's lens and project the pattern – say, leaves on a branch – on to the stage, giving the effect of being in a wood, forest or garden.

Lighting session
In some theatres, the lighting designer has the luxury of two separate sessions in which to first focus and then build each lighting state, but

more commonly they have just the one session in which to do both. Focusing cannot be carried out until the set is in place and has been dressed by the design and stage-management teams. Only then can the lighting team ascertain the effect that the lights will have and counter any negative reflections or glare produced. To focus the lights, the designer remains onstage while the deputy or assistant accesses the light by ladder or tallescope. The light will then be adjusted using the tilt and pan controls until it shines at the correct angle and with the correct beam intensity. At this point the lantern will be 'locked off' – the tilt and pan screws and the focus controls tightened so that they cannot slip – and the team will move on to the next lantern. Where general cover is being focused, the designer will walk a section of the stage, checking for dropout – unnatural areas of shadow that destroy the effect of one wash of colour. This is usually due to a badly positioned light and will need correcting before the session can continue. This is done on a regular basis to prevent the fault being discovered at the end of the session when it might be much harder to correct.

Once the lights are focused, the designer will begin to create lighting states cue by cue, introducing each lighting channel, adjusting the level of the lighting until they are happy. This lighting state will then be plotted, or where a computerised lighting desk is used, programmed in, ready for use in the technical rehearsal to follow.

How the lighting system works

It would be highly impracticable for each lantern to have its own very long power cable, which, once the designer had decided where to put it, was then trailed around the theatre before being plugged into a separate plug and operated individually. A production might require twenty or thirty lighting cues each consisting of several lanterns, and one person could not turn on or off so many plugs!

For this reason something known as a patch system is used. A patch system is made up of a mains power supply, a series of dimmers, a patch bay, the control board, a series of circuits or channels and the lanterns themselves, which are secured to a lighting rig.

Mains power supply

As we have seen, stage lanterns use far more power than domestic lights, so to power a lighting system, electricity is drawn directly from the National Grid through a series of powerful mains fuses, usually found in the systems distribution box. There will also be some form of trip switch that allows for circuits to be tripped or shut down where they are overloaded or faulty. This is also where the main switch that powers the lighting system is found.

Dimmers

Dimmers can be either portable or fixed and increasingly are found in analogue and digital configurations. The analogue dimmer is usually located in the distribution box alongside the mains power supply and the patch bay. A dimmer channel powers each lantern according to the voltage supplied via the lighting desk. Hence, as a fader on the lighting desk is raised, voltage increases in the dimmer, which increases the power supplied to the lantern, which in turn increases the intensity of the light it produces. Analogue dimmers usually contain a set of six paired sockets on a front panel, into which one of the circuits from the patch bay will be plugged; the newer digital dimmers achieve the same effect using binary computer coding. With the digital dimmer, numbers replace voltage to control the intensity of light, and because these numbers range from 0, which equals off, to 255, which equals fully on, much more precision in effect can be realised.

Patch bay

This is usually in the same place as the dimmers and the mains power supply and consists of a series of numbered plugs on three to four feet of cabling, suspended in a rack and connected, unseen, to each of the lighting circuits in the rig. The number on the plug represents one of the numbered circuits in the grid, and by patching this plug into one of the dimmer channels, that circuit and its lantern can be controlled by the lighting desk.

Control board

The control board, or lighting desk, allows for complete control of all the lanterns installed in the lighting rig, via a system of sliding switches known as faders. There are two types of lighting desk in use today: manual systems and memory boards. The older manual systems will offer a series of faders, which control channels, each channel representing a lantern or series of lanterns. By raising the fader to a numbered level, the intensity of the light produced by the lantern(s) increases or decreases. Rather than operate each channel separately, manual boards have master faders that allow a series of channels to be set at a variety of levels which are not put into effect until the master fader is raised. Additional features include timing dials which will implement the fader being raised or lowered across a given time span. Most manual boards will offer more than one pre-set; in other words there will be two banks of faders, one above the other, and each representing the same channel of the dimmer. This system allows the lighting operator to set up and implement one cue on the upper set of faders, while preparing the next lighting cue on the lower set, using the master fader to move between the two cues.

The memory board uses a computer system to store the number of the circuit used, the level of light required from that circuit and the sequential number of the lighting cue. During the performance, each cue is operated by the pressing of a single button, while a specialist software program implements the desired lighting effect.

Lighting rig

Above the stage there are a series of steel bars containing a number of cables, each cable being connected to a socket mounted on the external surface of the bar. Each socket represents a lighting circuit, and the cable connected to it runs back to the patch bay. By plugging a lantern into socket 35 (circuit 35) for example, and then placing plug 35 from the patch bay into channel one of the dimmer, raising fader number one on the lighting desk will bring up the lantern just installed.

Technical rehearsal

During the technical rehearsal, each cue will be confirmed in the prompt book and written on to the lighting cue sheet detailing which channels are being used, at what level and in what manner. For example, a 'snap blackout' requires the dimming of all the lights immediately, whereas a 'slow fade' requires a gradual reduction, the timing of which will be established during the technical. Where a computerised desk is being used, this process is carried out digitally. The channel and their levels are installed in the computer's memory along with any timings or effects required.

Throughout the technical rehearsal the lighting designer will sit in the auditorium with the director and other designers to see how their design works. They will make notes on any changes or alterations they feel are necessary and pass these on to the chief electrician, who will see that they are implemented by the dress rehearsal

Dress rehearsals

For the lighting team the dress rehearsals should be final confirmation that the design works and is effective, with only small alterations in cue timings and positions required. The designer will continue to make notes where necessary but, unless there are any significant technical difficulties, these will be minor.

The run

The previews offer the lighting operator the opportunity to establish their daily routine, which will be based around the production notes from the previous performance and the technician's own awareness of best practice. During the day, the lighting operator, who is usually the deputy chief or assistant electrician, will have other duties, but because they are also scheduled to work in the evening, they have a strict system of hours they can work. It is never a good idea for a tired technician to be climbing a ladder twenty-five feet up a rig having worked non-stop for twelve hours! During the day, a lighting operator will implement any significant lighting notes from the stage manager's report, and these might include replacing a gel that the DSM has spotted burning or smoking, or fitting a replacement bulb which has either blown or begun to dim – a good sign that the bulb is about to go.

Following a rest period prior to the performance, and an hour before 'the half' – the call that is made half an hour before the DSM warns beginners of the start of the performance – the lighting rig is 'powered up', or turned on. The operator will usually conduct a 'chase' of the lights, a facility available on both manual and computerised boards, where each of the channels in use is lit in turn so that the operator can check the lantern is working and that the bulb is good.

At the half, the lighting operator will implement any 'preset' – a lighting state already present as the audience enter the auditorium – before giving the DSM the lighting clearance. This tells the DSM that lighting has no further need of the stage and that they are production-ready. It is vital that the operator does this, as the DSM will not let the house manager open the auditorium to the audience until they have received clearance from all departments.

Strike and get-out

At the get-out, all the lanterns not required for the following production must be taken down from the rig. The strike usually starts straight after the last night of the production, but the lighting de-rig cannot take place immediately because the lanterns will still be very hot from the performance. Instead, while the set is struck, the lighting team will 'power down' the rig by switching off the dimmers, turning off the lighting desk and unpatching all the channels in the patch bay. Once cooled, the lanterns can be removed by unplugging them from the rig, removing the safety chain and the G clamp, and returning the light to its vertical position beneath the yoke. The lanterns are temporarily placed on the stage, standing on their faces, before being returned to storage.

Finding out more

Bell, Robert, *Let There be Light: Entertainment Lighting Software Pioneers in Conversation*, Entertainment Technology Press, 2004
Briggs, Jody, *Encyclopedia of Stage Lighting*, McFarland & Co., 2003
Fraser, Neil, *Lighting and Sound*, Phaidon Press, 1994

Morgan, Nigel H., *Stage Lighting Design in Britain: The Emergence of the Lighting Designer 1881–1950*, Entertainment Technology Press, 2005
Morgan, Nigel H., *Stage Lighting for Theatre Designers*, Herbert Press, 1995
Reid, Francis, *Lighting the Stage*, Entertainment Technology Press, 1995
Staines, Jackie, *Lighting Techniques for Theatre-in-the-round*, Entertainment Technology Press, 2000

CHAPTER 9

The sound designer

In the last few decades, advances in audio technology have given rise to the sound designer, a role that previously did not exist. Sound effects have been part of live theatre since the time of the ancient Greeks, and for hundreds of years remained essentially the same – the thunder machine used in Victorian and Edwardian theatres would have been recognisable to an ancient tragedian. The introduction of electricity and recordable media – first vinyl records and then electromagnetic tape – broadened the range and quality of sound effects available, but the role of the sound department was essentially the same: read the script, make a list of the sound effects described in the stage directions, check the director's requirements and then record them on to tape for use in the production.

What technology has done is allowed for diversification and sophistication within sound design and to make it part of the creative interpretation. Crossover from the commercial rock and pop industry means that techniques developed for high-end recording studios can now be effectively employed to enhance and develop the staging of a play. Sound – alongside set, costume and lighting – now seeks to create the world of the play, to immerse the audience in a series of sensory experiences that support the reality of the play.

Jobs in sound

Sound designer

A relatively recent addition to the creative team, the sound designer is often a musician or recording technician with a good grasp of modern recording technologies. They work on a freelance basis and may have a pre-existing relationship with the director and work with them on a regular basis.

Head of sound

In many producing theatre companies, the head of sound has been part of the electrics department, but as sound and sound technology becomes increasingly complex, most companies today have a separate sound team. The head of sound's chief responsibility is to maintain the audio equipment within the building, which will include the front-of-house audio equipment, the communication system backstage and the PA equipment, and to run a small team of staff who prepare and run the sound for each production the company presents. Sometimes the head of sound will also be the sound designer on a show.

Sound technician

Depending on the size of the theatre company and the number of spaces they operate, there may be one or several sound technicians. In larger buildings, a sound technician might have an area of expertise such as mixing or foley. Foley is a term borrowed from film and it's used to denote the person responsible for sourcing and recording sound effects for productions. Once the sound designer has identified the sound effects and music that she or he wants for the production, it will be the technician's job to source it in its raw state, before it can be edited or blended together to create the effect the designer wants. The technician might also create sound effects and music where none already exists.

Sound operator

Usually a career starting point, the sound operator will be responsible for operating the mixing desk and cueing the sound effects during the performance. They will also carry out day-to-day maintenance checks on the sound equipment, the stage-management communications system and the front-of-house intercom system.

Musical director

If live music is required, the director of the production will also hire a musical director, or the sound designer might also be a musical director. A freelancer, the musical director will create or make an arrangement of any scored music required. They will also audition and hire any musicians the production will need. Musical directors tend to be specialists – some work regularly in musical theatre, others in concert arenas, while some work specifically in straight theatre.

Production process

Pre-production

As one of the creative team, the sound designer comes on board in the early stages of the production process, and to begin with they will draw up a sound plan after reading the script several times. They will have had detailed discussions with the director beforehand and then will present their ideas to the director throughout the planning process.

The director and the sound designer may have worked together several times before, or it might be a new collaboration – some sound designers come from other art forms, such as opera, rock or pop, and are commissioned on the strength and style of their reputations in these forms, while others will cross over into theatre out of a desire to explore other media.

Today, the goal is often a total soundscape, the aural equivalent of a set or a costume – a creative interpretation of the play from a sound point of view. Sound in theatre has several different functions. First, most basically and where necessary, the actors' voices may need amplification so that they can be heard by all. Then there are sound effects, also know as spot effects – the sound of a dog barking, a car pulling up – although contemporary sound designers prefer to integrate such spot effects into overall soundscapes. The most subjective aspect of the sound designer's work and the newest and most inventive element is the creation of these soundscapes, born out of a traditional function of sound in theatre: the creation of atmosphere. Soundscapes can be used as transition effects from one scene into another, but increasingly they are being used like soundtracks in film, as a constant background to a scene, and modern technology makes this a much simpler task than it was in the recent past.

Principles of sound reproduction

Exploring the principles and processes of sound reproduction could fill an entire book, and it's not possible to give a thorough explanation of it here. However, it is important to grasp the basics in order to understand the role and function of sound in the live theatre and the principles on which the sound team are working.

Sound is created by an object vibrating, and these vibrations in turn travel through space in pressure waves. The disturbance they cause to the air around them creates a sound, and different sounds have different frequencies – human beings can hear sound frequencies between 15 and 20 kHz, but some animals can hear frequencies as high as 1,000 kHz. These pressure waves are not continuous and lose energy as they move through the air. In order to reproduce any sound in the artificial environment of the theatre, a means of recording and replaying the sound, or something like it, must be found. This is achieved by converting sound waves into an electrical signal that can reproduce the sound wave on demand. There are currently two methods of doing this: analogue and digital.

Analogue sound

The analogue-sound process was developed in the early days of the twentieth century alongside the advances in electricity and the new technologies it gave rise to. In the analogue process, sound waves are converted via a microphone into electronic signals that mimic the volume and duration of the original in a physical form, either as grooves on a vinyl record, or later as a pattern of magnetised signals on an audiotape. The process is not precise, and over time the media on which such sounds are stored can degenerate or be destroyed. Another drawback is that re-recording the sound on to another record or tape causes deterioration in the quality of sound from the original.

Digital sound

With the advent of computing and computer technology, the possibility of digital-sound reproduction was introduced. In digital-sound reproduction, the sound waves recorded by the microphone are converted into a series of binary codes that carry information about the frequency, the volume and the duration of the sound. The advantage of this form of sound reproduction is its lack of degeneration or distortion. Its faithfulness to the original source sound and the ability to manipulate the sound in many different ways are also advantages, plus large amounts of sound data made this way can be stored relatively easily with little fear of deterioration.

Rehearsals

While the cast rehearse, the sound designer and team will set about putting the sound plan into operation.

Sourcing sounds

Today there are two basic methods for acquiring spot sound effects for use in productions. One is via a sound and music library, which holds vast catalogues of sounds from the most common to the weird and wonderful. Many of these libraries can be accessed online, with tools that allow you to listen to a sample of the sound, pay for it by debit or credit card and download it directly to a computer for immediate use, replacing the old system of sound effects records and CDs.

Alternatively, the effect can be created and recorded from scratch, and this is often necessary when the sound is too production-specific to be found in a library. Sometimes it may be the case that two or three effects need to be layered in such a way that they can only be created from new. In such an instance, the sound technicians will experiment until they find a way of making the sound effect convincing. For example, if a production requires the sound of a beheading it is unlikely that any real recording of such an event will exist, so the sound team will experiment – knives and small cleavers are used to chop different fruit and vegetables in this case and recorded until the right sound is acquired! Creating the right sound effect can often lead to all sorts of weird and wonderful solutions, which might see the sound technician wading through jelly, or boiling kettles in buckets; it's whatever it takes to get the right sound.

Recording sound

At its simplest, the recording process channels sound from a source – a person, object or device – into a microphone and on to a recordable medium such as a computer hard drive, a tape or a CD-ROM.

Microphones

Microphones mimic the human ear in that they pick up sound waves travelling through the air and convert them into signals, the difference being that microphones use electricity to do this.

A microphone is composed of two elements: a capsule that holds the diaphragm – a taut membrane which vibrates under the pressure of the sound waves – and an attached transducer, which converts these pressure waves into electronic signals. Microphones vary in size and function and some require batteries (remote wireless mikes) or a nearby power source.

Recording devices

There are a variety of media on to which sound can be recorded, and as we have already established this can be via digital or analogue machines. From the 1940s analogue sound for theatre was mostly recorded on to magnetic tape via a reel-to-reel tape recorder. Strips of tape containing the required sound would be 'spliced' together, separated by coloured 'leader tape' containing no sound. When this leader tape travelled across the tape machine's 'play head' it would automatically stop, leaving the tape in the correct position for the next cue. This was a labour-intensive and imprecise method. Every time the same sound was required it had to be re-recorded and placed in the correct order on the tape, because the format didn't allow for quick or easy rewind. The 1970s saw the introduction of cart machines via the broadcasting industry, which used them for adverts and jingles. Cart machines used short continuous loops of tape that could be set up to either play continuously or once only, allowing more flexibility in sound cueing. Sounds needed to be recorded only once, and could be reused at will.

In the 1990s a new technology was introduced that would revolutionise the way sound was recorded and played back. The digital compact disc is a thin aluminium disc trapped between sandwiches of clear polymer. The blank disc is then etched using a laser, in much the same way that a needle once etched grooves in a vinyl record, but the precision of the laser, and the fact that the surface of the CD is protected by the polymer, means that damage and degradation is minimal. Tracks on a CD-ROM are searchable and can be precisely cued, offering ultimate flexibility to the sound operator. But the most flexible of all devices, and the most recent, is the hard disk recorder. Again transitioning into the theatre from the professional music industry, the hard disk recorder is high in memory capacity, allowing for the storage of large quantities of sound effect. It can be used in conjunction with a sampler, a device that allows a sound to be manipulated and changed, and once recorded the sound does not need to be moved on to another medium for use during performance – it can simply be accessed directly by a computer and sent as an output to an amplifier.

Mixing desk

Once sounds have been sourced and recorded, they will be edited and designed for playing during the performance, and this process is facilitated via the mixing desk. Put simply, a mixing desk allows sound from several different devices to be inputted through a series of channels where that sound can be modulated and altered before either being outputted on to a recorded medium, or replayed via amplifiers around the auditorium. In this way a CD player, a hard disk recorder and two or three microphones can be plugged into a mixing desk. Each will have a channel of its own, and on each channel the sound operator will be able to alter the sound by use of a range of dials that can change the bass or treble notes of the sound, and the balance between each of these two tones. The volume of a sound can also be changed via the mixing desk, so that while three different sound sources might enter the desk at the same volume level, they can be outputted at different levels to create a specific effect,

The output section of a mixing desk can vary according to its size and sophistication. The most basic mixing desk might have, say, eight input channels and two output channels, the minimum output required to create stereo sound. In professional theatres, the mixing desks would have far more inputs, perhaps twenty-four inputs as well as a group of sub-master channels, channels to which one or more input can be sent to create an effect which can be outputted to a specific loudspeaker or set of loudspeakers in the auditorium, allowing for the directionality of sound. For example, if the designer wants the audience to think a sound is travelling through or around the recording space, the input of this sound can be channelled to each of the sub-masters in turn, so that the sound will be replayed sequentially, making it appear that the sound is travelling.

The mixing desk is also used during the editing phase of the recording process, as different sound sources can be brought into the desk and layered and mixed to create effects that can then be sent back to the hard disk as finished cues, ready for the technical rehearsal.

Get-in and fit-up

While the lighting crew rig the lights, the sound team will be checking the sound equipment in the auditorium, moving speakers where required and setting up the mixing desk and computing ready for the technical rehearsals. Sound and lighting operators used to work in special booths or boxes high up in the auditorium overlooking the stage, and in some cases still do, but because equipment is no longer noisy and can be operated without disturbing the audience, and also because sound and lighting changes depend increasingly on more and more subtle cues, the sound desk is often situated at the back of the stalls or lower tier of the auditorium. Once the equipment is in place and cabled up, the connections will be tested to ensure everything is correctly wired and working, and then sound cues and volume levels will be checked through.

Sound plotting session

In this session the sound designer will work with the operator, the production's director and the DSM to establish where, when and at what volume each of the sound effects or soundscapes will be used. The sound operator will have prepared a sound cue list in advance, together with a number of sound cue sheets on which they can record the instructions, as they are decided. Increasingly, the need for cue sheets is being replaced by the use of computerised cue lists, but there are some operators who prefer a paper backup as security.

Technical rehearsal

For the sound team, the key value of the technical rehearsal is the integration of their work with that of the other design elements. It is during the technical that the sound operator will be able to find out if volume levels are too loud or too quiet, or whether a recorded effect is too long, too short or the appropriate length. It is only at the end of the technical rehearsal that the sound plot will be confirmed and locked into the computer ready for the performance.

The run

The preview period of a production will be used by the sound team to fine-tune the design, test the volume levels and make sure that it is having the desired effect on the audience. On a daily basis throughout the run, the sound operator will arrive before the show to carry out pre-show checks, making sure all the sound equipment is working and in the right place – speakers might have been moved by technicians working on part of the set or lighting rig, machines unplugged for use somewhere else, etc. They will also play through all the sound cues to ensure that they are in the right order and at the right volume level for the performance.

Strike and get-out

At the end of the production, the sound team will, where computerised cues are being used, download the sound for the show on to a recordable medium such as a CD for storage, before wiping the hard disk and computer memory. They will then de-rig all the sound equipment that is not permanently kept in the auditorium and put it back in the sound store, clear the sound operating station, return hired equipment and disconnect the inputs from the mixing desk. In this way the station is ready for the next production.

Finding out more

Coleman, Peter, *Basics – A Beginner's Guide to Stage Sound*, Entertainment Technology Press, 2004

Coleman, Peter, *Basics – A Beginner's Guide to Special Effects*, Entertainment Technology Press, 2005

Finelli, Patrick, M., *Sound for the Stage*, Entertainment Technology Press, 2002

Kaye, Deena, *Sound and Music for the Theatre: The Art and Technique of Design*, 2nd edn, Focal Press, 2000

Leonard, John A., *Theatre Sound*, A & C Black, 2001

Palmer, Scott, *Essential Guide to Stage Management, Lighting and Sound*, Hodder & Stoughton, 2000

Walne, Graham, *Sound for the Theatre*, A & C Black, 1990

CHAPTER 10

The marketing department

In today's media-savvy environment and with more and more demands on consumers' leisure time, the role of marketing in theatre is vital. Good marketing develops an audience and in turn that audience builds a relationship with the theatre. They trust its quality and its artistic output and come to rely on the fact that when they commit to buying a ticket, they will receive an entertaining night at the theatre.

Jobs in theatre marketing

Marketing director

The marketing director is a senior manager and will have considerable experience of arts marketing. Some will also have marketing or arts administration qualifications and they will be expert at dealing with the many aspects that make up the marketing department's job, most notably the pressure that is often part of launching a new season or production. They will draw up the department's annual marketing plan and policy; liaise closely with the artistic director via senior manager meetings to determine the content and 'look' of a season. They are responsible for the theatre company's image and profile both locally and nationally, and most of all they are responsible for seeing that their department stays on budget and meets the box-office targets set for each show. The marketing director must also analyse and process various forms of data concerning the profile of the company's audience, and utilise these data to gauge which of the company's productions will appeal to which sectors of the audience.

In some theatre organisations the marketing director is also responsible for the box-office department because its work is so directly connected to that of marketing.

Press officer

It is the press officer's job to see that the department's strategy for raising the profile of the production is implemented. The press officer develops relationships with local and national arts editors on magazines, newspapers and broadcast media networks in the hope of persuading them to conduct interviews with a production's leading actors and director, or to feature the production in their arts coverage. They issue production press releases that outline key elements of the production and its creative team, and also handle photo calls and photo opportunities, as well as any special promotions that accompany the show. On opening night, the press officer will meet the theatre critics who are reviewing the show. They will be given a ticket, a programme and an updated press release.

Marketing officer

The marketing officer's chief job is to see that the production is promoted through every avenue possible, and that the publicity required to achieve this promotion is ready on time and of a high standard. They will supervise the printing of posters, leaflets and programmes as well as ensuring that these are circulated. They negotiate advertising with various print media, and are responsible for all the direct mailing the theatre carries out. Internally, it is also the marketing officer's job to ensure that staff in other departments meet marketing-related deadlines, such as copy deadlines for material to be included in brochures and programmes.

Marketing assistants

In large marketing departments there may also be one or two marketing assistants, often trainees, who will take on a variety of duties as determined by the marketing director. This will often involve supporting either the marketing or press officer, as well as familiarising themselves with the day-to-day business of box office.

Graphic designer

Large theatre companies usually employ an in-house graphic designer/artist whose job it is to design the promotional material for each production, from poster to programme. Smaller companies will contract out this work to a graphic design company. Their specialist skills mean that they will work in collaboration with the marketing director, sourcing potential production images from stock photo libraries, suggesting appropriate fonts and layouts, and generally ensuring that anything written or printed that is sent out by the theatre company is in the correct style, from letterheads to purchase orders.

Production process

Pre-production

Before the production begins, the marketing team will plan the marketing strategy for the show. To do this they will analyse the SPs, or selling points, of the play, and cross-match this with the information they have about the audience from their audience-profiling statistics. This exercise will produce a target audience and give the team some idea as to which types of marketing will appeal.

The marketing director will have previously established how many tickets must be sold, and the team will now use that figure, together with the statistics they have worked out regarding the type of audience who might want to see the show, to work out how many tickets they must sell to each sector of their audience. For example, if the figures suggest that the production will appeal mostly to an audience over thirty, who attend the theatre regularly and who prefer more expensive seats, the marketing strategy for the production will focus on this audience. Of course, a good marketing strategy will target more than one audience, to improve chances of a full house, or a sold-out show. Once the audience profile for this particular production has been established, the team can then decide what sort of activities, events and promotions will appeal. So during pantomime season, events might focus around children, with competitions to draw characters from the show, as well as photo opportunities featuring well-known characters from the show – the Ugly Sisters for example. All of this will be written up into the marketing strategy and each element of that strategy will be assigned a series of deadlines in relation to the production itself, i.e. it's not possible to arrange a photo shoot with the Ugly Sisters until their costumes are finished.

The press officer will draw up the production press release as soon as the show is cast, and circulate it to their press contacts, while the marketing officer will ensure that print material is delivered and ready for distribution. The schedule of direct mailings will have already been determined and many of these will occur during the pre-production period.

First rehearsal
At the first rehearsal the marketing team will attend the presentations by the creative team in order to give them a better idea of how to talk about the production. They will listen to the read-through and socialise with the cast and crew to get a feel for those who will be most comfortable meeting and talking to the press. It's surprising, but not all skilful actors are also good at giving interviews or answering questions, and some will actively state that they do not give interviews and the press officer must respect the actors' wishes in these instances and find an alternative means to achieve their desired ends.

Rehearsals
While rehearsals continue, the marketing department maintains a busy schedule promoting the production, monitoring how well it is

selling and liaising with pressurised members of the production team to arrange interviews and visits from photographers.

Technical week
By this point most of the marketing department's pre-promotional work is done. However, for the press officer this is the ideal point at which to arrange interviews with actors. While the technical aspects of the show are put into place, the actors become more available. The press officer will arrange these interviews in consultation with those actors who have agreed to do them, and will ascertain from the journalists what sort of interview they want – it might be a one-to-one interview, or a group interview with several actors. The press officer will also arrange interviews for radio programmes or local TV shows, and as these often take place at the radio or TV studios, the press officer will accompany the actors as support.

The press officer will also arrange a photo call for the local and national press. The press officer, together with the director and marketing director, will pick interesting and significant moments from the play, which they will stage so that photos can be taken. The theatre will also have its own production photographer, who will take pictures during one of the dress rehearsals. These photos will be sent to the marketing director as a contact sheet, and half a dozen or so shots will be chosen for display in the venue's foyer area. One or two of these images might also be issued in the press pack for press night, and while some newspapers and magazines will use the photos issued by the theatre company, others prefer to take their own shots.

Previews
A member of the marketing team will endeavour to watch each preview, to monitor the developments in the production and to gather material on the performances that can then be written up into any follow-up press releases or additional copy.

Opening night
The focus of the opening night is the press officer, as this is the culmination of their role. A special desk is set up for the press, and the press officer or their assistant will be on hand to greet the critics as they arrive, hand them their press pack, containing their ticket, programme and press release, together with production photos and practical information they might need when writing their review. The press officer does not attempt to tell the critic what to write. Instead, they use a range of skills to put the critic at their ease, talk about the production in a positive light, and find ways of introducing useful information about the production and its progress. This is where the

hours spent in rehearsals and previews pay off, as critics are always searching for interesting anecdotes and comments that will make their review stand out from the others.

The run

Throughout the run, the marketing director monitors the daily box-office reports, indicating how many tickets have been and are being sold. In this way the team can determine whether they are on course to meet or exceed their box-office target. Often the team have already moved on to the next production, but the current one cannot be completely ignored. Where box office is slow, additional events, promotion and mailings may need to be organised, and there could be ongoing requests for interviews, which might continue until the final week of production.

The press officer will collect copies of anything that appears in newspapers, magazines and on television about the production, including reviews. These are posted daily on the production noticeboard. The marketing officer will monitor the success of advertising and promotion, usually by collating data gathered by the box office as people buy their tickets and are asked how they heard about the show.

Strike and get-out

Once the production is over, the marketing team must ensure that all print material for that production is removed from displays, both inside the venue and wherever else it has been distributed. Posters must be taken down from inside and outside the theatre and from advertising points around the local area – and nationally where a production has been so marketed.

Reviews and news clippings will be collated into a press production file and added to the company's archive, while the box-office takings and any audience data gathered will be put together in the production's marketing report which the marketing director will share with the artistic director and the other heads of departments.

Other forms of marketing

Design and brand

Just as in any other business with a product to sell, the theatre company must develop its brand, a unique identity that is easily recognised by a certain target audience. The brand is developed primarily by the artistic director and the head of marketing, and will stem from the company's artistic policy and the audience it would like to attract.

Image

The show's director and the head of marketing will discuss visual ideas and images that correspond to the director's interpretation of the play – the director with a view to communicating an idea of their production, the head of marketing with a view to making an impact on the right potential audience. Sometimes this image may be taken from a work of art, sometimes it will take the form of the title of the play itself and sometimes it will have to be shot, drawn or made specifically for the production.

Season brochure

Most theatre companies, whether they are producing just one show or a season of several shows, will issue a brochure providing details of the venues, dates and times of the performances, together with brief details of the play and its cast. A season brochure will also contain other information about supporting activities, and for building-based companies there will also be details relating to other departments, such as information about catering facilities, foyer events, opening times of bars, cafes and bookshops, as well as details of youth theatres and education activities. The majority of repertory companies will produce two seasons a year – a winter season and a spring season – as most theatres and theatre companies 'go dark', i.e. produce no plays, for the summer months.

Direct mailings and e-lists

Most regions of the country are now supported by sophisticated arts marketing organisations that can supply theatre companies with statistics regarding their potential local and national audiences. These organisations will often hold databases of members of the public who attend other theatres and have given permission for their details to be kept. These details can be bought and used as the basis for what is known as direct mail, the sending of letters, brochures and leaflets to a specific target audience the marketing department consider will be interested in a particular production. Databases are used to generate thousands of individual labels, which are then added to envelopes containing, for a season mailing, a new season brochure, a letter introducing the season and pointing out key highlights, together with promotional material from any visiting companies. Rather than individually posting such mailings, the mail is bundled up according to postal codes and bagged up awaiting collection from the postal service. In very large theatre organisations, the direct mailings are so huge that they are contracted out to specialist direct-mailing companies.

Theatre companies are making more and more use of the Internet in marketing, especially e-membership. Audience members submit their email details and sign up to the terms and conditions of the theatre's e-newsletter. This means that they receive an electronic version of newsletters, brochures and any other promotional material the company might issue. This is particularly useful for last-minute ticket deals and promotions, and serves as a more immediate tool for communicating with the company's audience.

Website

Websites are becoming powerful tools in the marketing of theatre companies and the promotion of productions, especially among younger audiences.

The website's function is similar to that of the season brochure, in that it aims to promote the company's productions, project an image of the company and its work, as well as keeping its loyal audience members informed of what's on. However, where the website scores over the brochure is that once the brochure is printed and mailed it cannot be changed or updated, whereas the website can.

Sponsorship and advertising

Theatre production is costly, and very few theatre companies can break even on ticket sales alone, so the marketing department will seek corporate sponsors for productions, particularly those productions that might offer a sponsor a good return for their investment. Sponsors make a gift of money towards a production or season in return for association with that season. This deal might include the sponsor's corporate logo being included on all the promotional material, or the season being named after the sponsor. It might also include a number of events to which the sponsor can invite their own guests and promote their own organisation in association with the theatre company and the production. Not all theatre companies can or want to attract corporate sponsors, and sponsorship has drawbacks as well as benefits, such as restricting a company's work.

Copywriting

This is an essential skill in marketing, and some companies will hire freelance copywriters in order to ensure its success. It is the ability to write about plays and productions in an interesting but succinct manner which will excite a target audience and prompt them to buy tickets.

Finding out more

Adkins, Sue, *Cause Related Marketing – Who Cares Wins*, Butterworth-Heinemann, 1999

Diggle, Keith, *Arts Marketing*, Rhinegold, 1994

Hill, Elizabeth, O'Sullivan, Terry, and O'Sullivan, Catherine, *Creative Arts Marketing*, 2nd edn, Butterworth-Heinemann, 2003

Kerrigan, Finola, Fraser, Peter, and Ozbilgin, Mustafa, *Arts Marketing*, Butterworth-Heinemann, 2004

Kotler, Philip, and Scheff Bernstein, Joanne, *Arts Marketing Insights: The Dynamics of Building and Retaining Performing Arts Audiences*, Jossey Bass, 2006

Mackowski, Chris, *The PR Bible for Community Theatres*, Heinemann Drama, 2002

Peithman, Steven, and Offen, Neil, eds, *The Stage Directions Guide to Getting and Keeping Your Audience*, Heinemann, 1999

Getting started

Sarah Hunt

I went to university and I did struggle about whether I should do a drama degree. But I thought you were an actor, or a writer, or a director, or a stage manager. I knew that that wasn't going to be enough for me, so with my boring hat on, I decided to rule that out and I applied to read English. And even then I struggled, I deliberately picked a very artsy college and thought, 'I'll read English, and I will go to the drama society; I'll be in London and I'll do all that and go and do theatre.' The drama society was actually full of really pretentious hideous 'drama' people and I couldn't get involved with them. And then, in the summer, I went up to the Edinburgh Festival and I worked with the National Youth Music Theatre for two or three years on the trot, starting off literally just before the festival. I thought I was going to hate it, but their commitment – they were so talented – it was just really inspiring, the buzz that you get, overhearing the audience having a good time and seeing how it all worked.

I finished my three-year degree and then got a job as senior box-office assistant, which basically meant that I did more hours than anybody else, not that I was senior in any way. The funny thing is my team were people like Dominic [Hill] who's now the director of Dundee Rep, and Rachel Kavanaugh, who's artistic director of Birmingham Rep. They were my box-office team!

Then the marketing person took sick leave for six weeks and so I, at no extra money, was asked – well, it was presented to me as an opportunity – to help with the marketing, which, again, I just worked really stupid hours so that I could do that in order to put it on my CV. I knew it was my first job, so you don't want to be sniffy, and in a theatre that size it gets noticed really quickly.

The only thing I did at the same time was a part-time post-graduate diploma in arts management, which was two evenings a week. So, every evening I was either at the theatre or at college – I had Sunday evening off to myself – and they were some of the best years of my life. I then applied to be the marketing assistant at the English Touring Opera. It was a really, really good maiden job and, again, I was encouraged to have a sort of a good overview, to look and to listen and to just soak up. If you want to, in a job like that in a small theatre, you can learn so much. So I did that. And I worked for three years at English Touring Opera which was fantastic in that it was a touring opera company. I had to learn about deals and cultures, and my manager was incredibly good.

Then, after four years there, I was employed as the marketing manager at the Tricycle Theatre. I stayed four years and actually that was a big step for me at the start. They built a 300-seat cinema and I oversaw the project. There was a really, really good children's programme, education programme, as well. We had an art gallery and the cinema, we were very much doing work for the community, lots of Irish plays and plays by black writers, and my job was making sure that the marketing campaign worked. So my four years there were a mixture of everything in marketing. Amazing! And then the Tricycle closed for refurbishment and I became the marketing director at the Donmar Warehouse, where I worked for three years producing pretty much everything.

There were two really exciting things. I worked a lot with New York, and either we had shows transferring to New York, or we had shows that would be in New York and transferring here. Like there'd be a co-production, and I'd never worked on a co-production before and that was fascinating. I also worked on a couple of West End transfers, which I hadn't worked on before, because I'd only ever worked in subsidised theatre, not in commercial theatre. This was the most commercial experience I ever had and, my God, it is more scary because you are responsible for marketing something on which someone has remortgaged their house!

After that I went to the Bristol Old Vic as head of marketing and then I got a call from the National Theatre who were creating this deputy director of marketing – sales and marketing – and so I have been here for just over a year now. And this is, again, another kind of thing; they have three theatres here – a 300-seat theatre, a 900-seat theatre and a 1,200-seat theatre – and we have two or three shows in each theatre. I work in rep and I've never worked in true rep before, and that's exciting. I've also gone on several tours, internationally and nationally. The marketing department – it is massive here.

I think marketing is about communication, being able to really listen and understand the passion of the play. I would never employ anybody who didn't go to the theatre, because every single person in our department goes about twice or three times a week. You want people who are totally abreast of what's going on in the world, you've got to engage with the world, and I mean on every level – political as well as social and cultural.

You need to have really good planning skills because that's what the job is. You're a coordinator, you have to have a good eye and you need a sense of what you all do and what sells physically, because, fundamentally, my job is to sell tickets. I've got find the right audience. I've got to understand what the play's about, know what audiences will go and see, so that I get a return on my investment. And that's the other thing, proper financial nous is essential – you've got to be able to budget, you've got to be able to stick to tight deadlines, you've got to be able to communicate, and you've got to be able to have attention to detail and enjoy it.

Let me start with a whole week. Monday, I'll meet the director of marketing. We'll go through the issues for the week – just the usual general administrative stuff but then I'll check every day to make sure everybody knows what they're doing, how they're doing it. There's always all manner of adverts and leaflets being prepared in the graphics department, so I'll go and check how they're getting on with those. On Friday we'll have a weekly marketing meeting with our agency, and that's when we go through all the shows, current and forthcoming, and we create the campaigns. And again, we look at the sales figures. We look at the sales figures on a daily basis, hourly on some shows, and just assess whether we've got the campaign right, or whether we need to knock it into another area.

What else would I like to do? I know what I don't want to do. I don't want to be a producer like a lot of marketing people want to. I'd quite like to be a general manager, I think. Actually, I want to be the director of marketing, that is one thing I'd like to do. The other thing I'd like to do is go and work in New York or Australia, I'd really like to do that. I don't know. I want to stay working here for another couple of years though. I've still got a lot to learn.

CHAPTER 11

The education department

It is commonplace today to find an education department in most producing theatre companies and buildings; even commercial theatre producers have come to see the importance of providing educational support for their key productions. However, the work of the education department is a relatively recent innovation in theatre, growing out of the new theatre movements of the late 1950s and 1960s. Today, the provision of an education programme and community projects is a requirement of Arts Council core funding.

There are an ever growing number of roles and functions in which the theatre educator can be employed. Larger producing theatres tend to have an education department with a number of employees, whereas touring theatre companies and independent producers may employ education professionals on a freelance basis, and some companies may rely solely on one education officer.

Jobs in theatre education

Education director

The education director or manager will be an experienced practitioner with significant knowledge of both education and theatre. Education directors are usually senior managers, and will meet with the company's artistic director and the other senior managers on a regular basis, to discuss the company's day-to-day work and plan forthcoming seasons. They also keep the artistic director up to speed with what's happening in their department and will advise on changes and trends in arts and education policies as they relate to the company and its work.

As well as managing their team of staff, the education director will be responsible for drafting and implementing the company policy on education and community work, as well as policy and guidance on child protection and working with young people and vulnerable adults within the company. This is especially relevant in building-based companies. These companies are community resources and as well as visiting schoolchildren there are also projects that might involve young people in other ways.

Education officer

The education officer will assist the education director in the running of the department and will often take on responsibility for planning and organising individual projects. The education officer will also be responsible for the drafting of resource materials such as production support packs for schools or notes for teachers. It is usually the education officer who coordinates freelance staff, ensuring that there are adequate numbers to cover the department's needs, and that the freelancers have the appropriate certification. The education officer is usually an experienced workshop practitioner and will be capable of leading workshops, although the rest of their workload may mean they seldom get the opportunity. In companies where there is no education director, it is often the education officer who will carry out the senior manager's duties instead.

Youth theatre officer

Today, many theatre companies offer a youth theatre to their local community, and this is particularly true of building-based companies. The youth theatre officer is the member of the education team who coordinates the youth theatre under guidance from the education director. This will include organising youth theatre sessions, choosing plays that the youth theatre will perform and overseeing the term-by-term membership of the youth theatre. The youth theatre officer will also usually direct the youth theatre productions.

Workshop leaders

On the whole, workshop leaders are freelance staff who are employed on a session-by-session basis. They will be skilled at preparing practical exercises that will help the participants understand key aspects of the play they have seen or are about to see. Experienced workshop leaders might also be employed as education project leaders, responsible for coordinating and supervising large projects in the community, putting together a series of workshops and events, and employing the appropriate staff to deliver them.

Chaperones

Chaperones are licensed by their local authority to care for children, specifically when they are taking part in live performances or film and TV recordings, and it is mandatory for a theatre to employ chaperones when children are engaged in a professional production. The chaperone can supervise a given number of children, and will look after them while they are not onstage, ensuring that they rest and take adequate refreshment. They will escort the children to and from the stage, and wait with them until they are collected from the theatre at the end of the performance.

Theatre tutors

This is another specialist role, most usually found in the large touring commercial productions where a number of children form part of the cast, e.g. *The Sound of Music*. The tutor will be a qualified state teacher and will be responsible for delivering curriculum sessions arranged around the rehearsal schedule and performances. In most cases, production companies and directors will attempt to work around a young person's schooling, rehearsing after school hours and at weekends, but sometimes this is not possible. At this point it becomes mandatory that the production employ a tutor.

Production process

Pre-production

Long before the season begins, the education department will have planned their programme of work, so that they can inform schools and colleges in good time. Organising school trips is a complex business and teachers often need at least a term's notice before they take pupils out of school to visit the theatre. With the support of the marketing department, the education department carries out regular mailings to schools and other educational institutions, setting out the education programme of workshops etc., giving information about the youth theatre and generally keeping them up to date on events. There will also be details on any special ticket deals and a season brochure included in this mailing.

The team will decide whether a production requires resources, and where this is the case, the education director or officer will supervise the drafting of the production's resource material, which might include information about the playwright and the play, a synopsis of what the play is about, as well as background information on themes in the play, the period it's set in or anything else that might be useful to the teachers and students attending a performance.

First rehearsal

The education director will usually attend the first rehearsal to introduce themselves to the cast and crew and outline the sorts of activities that are planned in support of the show. They will listen to the presentations made by the designer and other members of the creative team, as well as sitting in on the read-through in order to get to know the actors.

Rehearsals

During the rehearsal period itself, the education department continues to prepare resources, and will often sit in on several rehearsals to see how the production is developing. The education officer or another member of the team will conduct interviews with the director and cast which will be added to the resource material along with set designs and costumes sketches for example. As rehearsals draw to a close, the resource material will be made available to those groups coming to the performance.

In some theatre companies, the education department also has a responsibility for internal education or training programmes, meeting the needs of staff. This might include refresher courses for technicians, or regular skills classes in voice and movement for actors. Sometimes it might involve organising special masterclasses from practitioners visiting the area or working with the company on a project. This tends to be the case in companies where an ensemble of actors is hired for a whole season, often away from their homes and living in digs. At home they might take classes during the day to maintain their skills, and then give a performance in the evening.

The run

While the education department plays little part during technical week, once the play has begun its run there are a number of events that the education team can supervise.

Meet the cast

Many companies offer the opportunity for the audience to meet and question the cast and director of a production following one of the performances, and this event is often chaired by the education director.

Theatre days

It is the education department's responsibility to plan and run the theatre day, or play day. These are public workshops that usually take place prior to one of the matinee performances of the play. Unlike specialist schools' workshops, these are available to anyone with a ticket – often sold as part of a package for the matinee performance. Because these events can be well attended, and in some cases, with popular shows, may run to capacity, they cannot feature the sort of intimate participatory work of the schools' workshops. Instead, they will often consist of presentations by the director, designer or cast members, a demonstration of rehearsal techniques and the opportunity to engage the cast in a question-and-answer session. These workshops might also, health and safety allowing, be a chance for the audience to go onstage and explore the set from a unique perspective.

The education department will begin formulating ideas for this workshop in the early part of rehearsals and once the play is fixed, usually during technical week, the education director or officer will meet with cast and director to discuss possibilities and agree a format. This work is now a relatively common feature in theatres, so cast and director will often have taken part in them before. However, that's not to say there isn't a degree of anxiety, because the role that they must play is a mixture of performer and teacher, and while they are skilled at the former they may have no confidence in themselves as the latter. For this reason the workshop is led and coordinated on the day by a member of the education team, or a freelance animateur or workshop leader hired by the education department for the event. The aim of the theatre day is to give those attending a unique insight into the production. It helps develop a bond with the theatre or theatre company and makes them an appreciative audience during the performance.

Outreach projects

In addition to the work the education department does in support of the theatre company's repertoire, they will also devise and respond to community and educational initiatives by creating special projects that go out into the community, hence the term 'outreach'. The aim of this outreach work might be to use theatre skills and creativity to address a socially destructive problem, such as crime or substance abuse, or it might serve to help a group come together. Other initiatives might have a more formal educational emphasis related to the national curriculum or a directive from central government. In some cases the project will come from the education department, and address a need arising in their day-to-day work with the schools, colleges and community groups that make up their clients.

Other forms of educational theatre work

Theatre-in-education companies

Theatre-in-education, or TIE, developed in the late 1950s and early 1960s, to some extent from the work of Dorothy Heathcote and in particular the work done by the Belgrade Theatre in Coventry. They pioneered an innovative new method of making theatre for young people in the school-classroom context. This type of theatre was designed to educate and challenge pupils to ask questions. It was made not by actors, but by actor-teachers, many of whom had qualified from courses where a drama qualification was linked to their education qualification.

The most significant difference between them and their fellow actors was that they knew and understood the school curriculum and working practices. TIE plays were not just focused on English literature; they took as their subject any aspect of the curriculum – history, science, geography – seeking to bring subjects alive in the minds of young people. Companies such as those at Belgrade and Leeds Playhouse developed working practices drawn from some of the new drama theorists such as Augusto Boal and Jerzy Grotowski, as well as employing some of the techniques being developed by drama educators such as Gavin Bolton, Jonathan Needlands and the aforementioned Dorothy Heathcote. Most important of these was participation. TIE explores theatre as a process rather than as a final, finished product and, in doing so, allows the idea of change. Because the TIE company's audience participate in the drama, they make decisions within the drama that can affect the outcome. This means that performers have to be skilled in devising, and knowledgeable about the subject in hand, for if their young audience decide to take them on to a different aspect of the subject, they have to follow. Key means for involving their audience are the breaking down of the fourth wall. Much TIE happens in the round, in among the audience. Actors will often confide in their audience or, more importantly, encourage the audience to participate as equals. For example, in a piece of historical TIE about the suffragettes, a female actor playing a suffragette may encourage the part of the audience she is closest to to see themselves as fellow suffragettes and the opposite side of the audience as politicians preventing the suffragettes from having the vote. In this way, young people not only participate in the drama, but are able to empathise with the historical figures they are studying in a more visceral and immediate way than textual or didactic study. TIE was a very powerful force in the 1960s and 1970s, with most repertory companies across the UK employing their own TIE teams alongside the independent touring TIE companies, but the movement suffered greatly in the early 1980s under new Arts Council policies and government initiatives to drive down spending in the arts. Yet it is a most effective form of educational theatre, and as such was impossible to kill. The late 1990s and early twenty-first century has seen a resurgence in this sort of work, together with a whole new generation of practitioners using modern technology and teaching methodologies to develop the work still further.

Children's theatre
Unlike TIE, children's theatre takes place outside the educational context. Another development of the 1960s child-centred arts policies, it was recognised that there was great cultural benefit in creating theatre specifically for young people, addressing their issues

and concerns and exploring the fast-changing world from a young person's perspective. This might include plays about children's issues, such as divorcing parents, issues surrounding drugs, etc., but it might just as easily be an adaptation of a popular children's book or a wholly creative piece of work that is not in the least 'issue'-driven. The key here is that the work is for and about young people. Many theatre companies will stage young people's theatre at specific times of the year, most typically during school holidays, and there are some companies whose entire repertoire is based on plays for young people. The Half Moon is one example, presenting plays for young people from the ages of four to sixteen.

Young people's theatre and youth theatre
While children's theatre is made *for* young people, young people's theatre is made *by* young people. Primarily it is made by young people in youth theatres across the country, whether these are part of their local repertory theatre, or organised by the county council or local education authority. Some are independently run and there is an argument for adding to this category the youth companies developed by the growing number of commercial stage schools which are run after school and at weekends. The aim of most youth theatres is to engage young people in the theatre-making process, to develop their skills both in terms of drama but also in the social context, and to offer young people the opportunity to perform on a regular basis. Most will meet weekly and sessions will include games, improvisation and drama skills development. Older members of youth theatres will participate in productions, engaging in the same process as adult professionals, from auditions through rehearsals and on to performance. Many have the opportunity to be involved in backstage and technical capacities, and where the youth theatre is based in a professional producing theatre, the youth theatre will have the opportunity of performing on its stage to a paying audience. Many young people who participate in youth theatre go on to take a drama-related qualification and some go on to train as actors or technicians, as the experience is very useful preparation for a professional career.

Finding out more

Coult, Tony, and Kershaw, Baz, eds, *Engineers of the Imagination: The Welfare State Handbook*, revised edn, Methuen, 1990
Doyle, Rex, *Staging Youth Theatre – A Practical Guide*, Crowood Press, 1998
Fox, John, *Eyes on Stalks*, Methuen, 2002

Getting started

Jackie Skinner

I used to do ballet when I was three years old and my mum took me to the ballet, which I think was at Drury Lane or Covent Garden – I can't remember where – but that was my first experience of actually being in a huge auditorium, and I was absolutely captivated by it, even at that age, just completely entranced. Not just by what was happening on the stage, but the whole spectacle of it, and I think that was the thing, even at that age, which sowed the seed – it wasn't just going to be getting up and doing it that I was interested in, but the whole atmosphere and excitement.

I was from a very rural background, and then when I was eleven we moved to Horsham and I joined an amateur dramatics groups because my mum said I was very dramatic and I should be putting it to some good use! There wasn't really very much drama at school so I didn't really get into it until I was a bit older, but by that point I knew that all I wanted to do was theatre, or art and design, and in fact for quite a long time I wanted to be a set designer.

I was still interested in performing, but I started to learn about other jobs that you could do and for my A-level practical I didn't do an acting exam, I did set design. I was quite into surreal . . . I think I did a set design for *Kvetch*, a Steven Berkoff play, which is a kind of weird choice for a seventeen-year-old.

And then I took a year out, and this was the clincher because I deferred for a year and I went back to my old school. For a year I taught drama and I taught art, and I directed a play with the year tens.

My work-based learning project in the third year of my degree was working with recovering heroin addicts through drama, teaching them social skills to try and get them back into work or education. So quite a leap. But when I was a teenager I'd also helped run youth clubs and had that kind of interest in working with young people – and not only young people, I used to do visits to older people and just . . . I knew then that whatever I did it would be working with people. It had to be working with people. So I suppose from then on I was trying to think of ways that I could mould my interest in theatre and my interest in people. So I completely loved doing that project with the recovering drug users.

When I left university I worked for a couple of years on a graduate training scheme. We learnt computer skills, such as website design, and I was still involved in productions, but also with students, so it was kind of an interesting job to be in. I did a bit of tutoring at that point with first years which was great. And then . . . I didn't know, I was sort of stuck between the education side and the production side, which one do I go for?

Then I got my first job as production assistant at Derby Playhouse where I was in a busy production department and I just learnt everything. I used to watch every show from the director's box, from backstage, from the audience, from . . . every way I could watch a show I would. I was only there about eighteen months, but used it in every way I could to learn everything about how a theatre really works because I didn't . . . well, nothing against the degree course I did, but I didn't feel that I knew the theatre world after university and I was very aware, a lot of people had told me, 'Yeah, you can do a course,' but actually you need to know how it works in the real world.

I knew that I wasn't really interested in the 'luvvie' side of theatre. I was much more interested in what theatre could do for people. OK, so then I got a job managing a small-scale theatre company, and I wanted to do something involving productions because I still had my passion for theatre, but something also that was more about working with people and actually using the arts to bring the best out in people to develop their skills in some way.

Then I became education officer for Liverpool Everyman and Playhouse and that was brilliant, because through the MA I'd taken I'd had experience of working with people with mental health problems, older people, people with different physical and mental disabilities, people from lots of different ethnic backgrounds, and Liverpool Everyman and Playhouse gave me the opportunity to try out those methods all over again and to actually run projects. It's sort of gathering different strings to the bow, I think, all of it, and I think everything I did in those ten years between starting at Derby Playhouse and then starting at Liverpool Everyman and Playhouse was bringing all that together.

Theatre is always viewed as being very glamorous, but actually most of the jobs in it aren't very glamorous at all, and it was accepting that the joy I got from working in theatre didn't come from any kind of fake glamour or praise that I was getting for myself, but it was more from watching other people that I was working with achieve something, or come to a certain point of recognition about themselves or about what their situation, things like that.

Theatre is a hard thing to engage in. It's not necessarily something you can assume people know how to do. I certainly didn't. When I was a teenager, I spent twenty minutes looking at the set and by that point I'd kind of completely lost what was actually going on in the play, but I was so interested in how the set moved and everything like that, it was all I needed to know.

So most people in theatre, especially those who work in education, have a real passion for keeping it going and developing new audiences, and I don't just mean new audiences as in young people. I think part of it is teaching people how to 'read' theatre.

Then there's the whole other side of it which I'm really passionate about: the power of theatre and participation and the arts, that you can work with any group from any background. Theatre is about community and giving people a voice – I know it's become a bit of cliché now, but that's what it's about. Everyone has it within them to be creative, and for me it's about channelling that creativity into a product through a process and enabling people to do things that they never thought were possible. On the primary-school programme, we say to the children at the beginning: 'By the end of your six workshops you will be doing a performance in assembly and you will be acting or designing or whatever role you have within the team,' and they don't believe it, but the fact that they can achieve it within that time is absolutely mind-blowing for them and creates those kinds of experiences that you never forget and those kinds of experiences that I talk about now, at my age, which I remember from when I was three. Those kinds of first-engagement moments that kind of stay with you for ever and that's about personal development. It's not about some arty-farty side of theatre. It's actually about people.

CHAPTER 12

House management

Everyone who goes to the theatre experiences 'front of house'; indeed, for most of the audience, these are the only members of the theatre company, aside from the actors, they will encounter. This places the front-of-house operation on the front line of customer relations – a bad experience with a rude or unhelpful usher can colour your entire evening's experience, put you off the play or going to the theatre again. With so many leisure opportunities competing for people's attention, it is important therefore that the front-of-house team is friendly, well disciplined and expert in customer care.

The term 'front of house' is traditionally used to indicate everything that is not concerned with getting the production onstage and which takes place in front of the curtain or stage. In general it refers to the public areas of a theatre building, and all the departments and staff involved in them.

Modern house management is a complex mix of high-end hospitality work, retail and event management. Today's theatre buildings must work hard to earn their keep for the companies that run them. Some are listed buildings costing hundreds of thousands of pounds to maintain, while others are sprawling modern complexes with huge heating and lighting bills. The common denominator is that they are all public buildings and where once the manager would open the doors of a theatre one or two hours before a performance, and be assisted by one or two box-office clerks and a handful of ushers, shutting the doors again as the last member of the public left, modern theatres offer bars, restaurants, galleries, bookshops and a daily programme of activities, events and tours.

Jobs in front of house

Executive director

Larger theatre companies have, over the last ten years, begun to appoint executive directors alongside their artistic directors. Most have background as producers or house managers and their task is to look after the financial health of the company, ensuring that there is enough money being made or raised to fund all the productions to company plans, as well as paying the salaries of all those employed. In the subsidised theatre, this also means ensuring that grants and subsidies are spent wisely and proper accounts are kept. It's the executive director who will be involved in contracting the various artists who work for and with the company, as well as being responsible for raising funds for the company via sponsorship, charitable donations and 'friends' schemes.

House manager

The house manager, who is increasingly referred to as the general manager in larger theatres, looks after all of the front-of-house departments, either managing them directly or supervising other people to manage them. He or she will usually have worked as a duty manager before being promoted to house manager. It's their objective to ensure the public areas of the theatre work and are staffed effectively. The general, house or theatre manager has significant responsibility as they are in charge of health and safety within the building, the security of the public and staff working in the building, as well as looking after the access requirements of the general public, particularly those with disabilities, which might range from special audio loops for those with hearing difficulties, to access to the auditorium for wheelchair users or special described performance for blind patrons.

In a small venue, house managers may simply have responsibility for opening and closing the theatre and coordinating the ushering team; in a larger venue they might be responsible for the management of several sub-departments and dozens of staff.

The house manager may be one of the senior management team of a theatre company, and attend regular senior management meetings where the smooth running of front-of-house and backstage operations are discussed. In large producing companies, the house manager will be required to ensure no one operation and its events clashes with another, and they'll need to maintain effective shift systems so that performances are not under- or over-staffed.

The house manager must have a firm grasp of health and safety guidelines, since they relate to running a theatre and hosting members of the public, as well as being fully conversant with the theatre's insurance and public liability policies. In the event of an emergency or a security alert, the house manager is the named 'responsible person' who must safely evacuate public and staff without panic or injury. They must be familiar with fire regulations and ensure that each production and its set and costumes have been approved by the fire safety officer. They are also responsible for obtaining and enforcing the requirements of the company's theatre licence and music licence together with any licence the theatre holds for serving food and alcohol. The house manager must implement effective first aid strategy and ensure that there are qualified first aiders on duty every time the public are in the building. They ensure incidents are dealt with swiftly and calmly and that any accidents are recorded in the accident book.

The roles and responsibilities of a house manager are considerable, and only the most efficient and capable of individuals have the skills required for the job!

Duty manager

Now that many modern theatre buildings open from mid-morning to late evening, and the work of the house manager has become so broad and varied, duty managers are employed to manage the evening or matinee performance separately to the role of the house manager. This is mostly due to practicality of hours. If a general manager starts work at 9.30 a.m., he or she cannot be expected to work until 10 or 11 p.m. every day.

Head of box office

The head of box office is responsible for managing a team of mostly part-time staff, and coordinating the sale of tickets via the various outlets – in-person bookings, telephone bookings, agencies, groups and tickets bought online or by post.

Box-office assistants

Those who work as box-office assistants mostly do so on a part-time basis. Many are drama students, actors, directors or other theatre professionals, for whom part-time shift work is useful, giving them freedom to pursue auditions or other work. Assistants will work either at taking sales via the phone, or in the foyer selling tickets direct to the public. Some of the work will involve processing bookings that have been made via the theatre company's website or through ticket agencies around the country or abroad. A box-office assistant might also deal with group bookings.

Retail manager

The retail manager will look after any merchandise that the company sells, from T-shirts, posters and company memorabilia to programmes and scripts.

Retail assistants

Depending on the size of the theatre company and the building they occupy, retail assistants might be drawn from the ushering team, or may be employed separately, often because the point of sale they operate is open outside of performance times. Retail assistants might be employed permanently, for example to staff the theatre's bookshop, or on a part-time shift basis to run a kiosk that sells a range of merchandise but only for a set period around the performances.

Ushers
Most ushers are part-time members of staff who work three or four shifts a week, or more, depending on the time of year and the number of the performances being staged.

Catering manager
Depending on the size of the venue, the catering manager might also be the head chef or cook, or bar manager where there is no restaurant present. Some restaurants in well-known theatres have local and national reputations as places for fine dining and their chefs can be as renowned as those in starred and award-winning high street restaurants. In large theatres there will be a catering manager in addition to the head chef of the theatre's main restaurant operation. The catering manager supervises the shifts and workloads of all the catering staff, from waiters in the restaurant and/or cafe to the bar staff and sometimes those who sell sweets and ice creams during the interval.

Events manager
Some theatres today offer their spaces for hire to companies and individuals who might want to use them to launch a product, stage a conference or hold a party or wedding, so these theatres now employ events managers, mostly those who've gained experience in the hospitality industry in hotels or conference centres. Hiring the theatre or its spaces out cannot interrupt the production schedule, but for financially challenged theatres can offer lucrative opportunities.

Production process

Daily front-of-house routine
Because the front-of-house operation is not production-delimited, there is little point describing it from a production process point of view. Instead, it makes more sense to look at it from a daily basis, exploring some of the differences there are between days when there are no performances to days when there are evening performances only, or days where there are matinees and evening performances.

The daily routine of the front-of-house operation begins with cleaning up after the previous evening's performance. Most theatres will have a 'duty' stage-door keeper who will let the cleaning staff into the building before the house manager arrives. They will clean and vacuum the auditorium and the public spaces, as well as the staff offices and dressing rooms.

Daily front-of-house briefing

Where a building is open to the public throughout the day, the house manager will usually hold a daily briefing for the various heads of box office, catering, retail etc., to talk through any specifics of the day. This briefing allows front-of-house staff to be aware of each other's schedules – a large group of theatregoers may have booked a pre-matinee lunch, which will have implications on how many other patrons the restaurant can seat. A backstage tour may be taking place, or an education event – all these things will affect the front-of-house operation for the day. Once heads of departments have met they will then brief their teams before assigning them their tasks; because many theatres are now open for twelve or fourteen hours a day, staff work in shifts, each shift being responsible for different aspects of a department's work. The day shift in the box office will process any bookings taken via the website overnight, and process postal bookings that arrive in the morning, while the afternoon shift might process bookings that have taken place during the day. The chef who cooks lunch will not be the same chef who runs the pre- and post-show restaurant.

The house manager is responsible for checking that the building is ready to be opened to the public on time, and once the doors are open, she or he is ultimately responsible for their safety while inside the building.

Busy times for theatres are lunchtimes and the couple of hours immediately before a performance, and the hour after the performance ends. On days when there are matinees, these busy periods overlap, and it's the job of the house manager and their team to ensure that these periods pass off smoothly.

Productions often 'come down' or finish late in the evening. In theatres where there are bars and restaurants, patrons, cast and crew may often wish to have a drink or light meal after the show, which may mean that the theatre won't close until midnight.

Finding out more

Byrnes, William J., *Management and the Arts*, 3rd edn, Focal Press, 2003
Chong, Derek, *Arts Management*, Routledge, 2002
Hagoort, Giep, *Art Management: Entrepreneurial Style*, Eburon, 2001
Pick, John, and Anderton, Malcolm, *Arts Administration*, 2nd edn, E & FN Spon, 1996

Getting started

Rebecca Morland

I directed one play in a one-act play competition at university. We went through the entire period of rehearsals thinking it was a deep, tense tragedy, then halfway through the performance the audience started laughing. The actors turned to look at me in the wings and I realised at that moment I wasn't really meant to be a director. It was so sad! I went the whole way through university doing all the nuts and bolts. I produced shows, I stage-managed them, I got the publicity together, I was treasurer of the university dramatic society, I took plays to Edinburgh, etc. It wasn't until my third year that I actually realised there was a career called arts administration. I went along to the careers department and said, 'Arts administration?' They gave me a very thin folder and said, 'You can go and work at the BBC.' I said, 'No, I think I'm interested in theatre,' and they went, 'Oh . . . I'd do a secretarial course if I was you.'

I went to London because that's where I thought all the jobs were. I worked as an usherette in the evenings in the West End in a charming nylon overall. Eventually, I ended up as a PA to Ian Albery who ran, at that point, six West End theatres including the Donmar Warehouse. So I did that for about two and a half years and that was my first nuts-and-bolts, proper, paid-full-time, enough-to-eat, job. They were an old theatrical family. They got taken over by somebody while I was there and eventually he was bought out and I was made redundant.

I also got bored. It's a great West End job, being a PA to somebody who runs theatres or indeed to a theatre producer, as long as you don't mind not taking responsibility, and I started wanting to manage things a bit more. Ian was very supportive and got me some front-of-house management work at the Donmar, so I did a bit of that. And that meant that when it all sort of came to a halt there I had enough skills to apply for a job as a house manager. And then I went off to the Mercury Theatre, Colchester, as a front-of-house manager – that was my first management job.

In those days it was very old-fashioned. Front-of-house people ran box offices because nobody thought that box office were really part of marketing then. They were just people who sold tickets and who were nice to customers. So I managed the box office and I was front-of-house manager. I managed a team of usherettes, making sure they were on duty for every performance. I made sure that the sweetie and the ice-cream stocks were up to speed. And I was responsible for the health and safety and well-being of an audience, which is very scary when you're about twenty-five and in charge of several hundred people; getting them in and out of the theatre, making sure nothing horrible happens to them, and knowing what to do if the fire alarm goes off. It's a really tough job, house management – some people love it and do it for the rest of their lives and some people go, 'Ooh God!' I think it was pantos that broke me!

I went back to London and became administrator for the Soho Theatre Company, a new writing company, at that point based in offices over in Goodge Street and a small theatre in a cellar somewhere else in Soho. And I was administrator, which was brilliant; basic finance, basic contracts, basic admin. I started to find out about things like funding applications, and because it was a small company did a lot of really hands-on finance. Again, a very useful nuts-and-bolts position. By the time I'd finished with that I knew how to manage staff, I knew how to do contracts, I knew enough about finance and that meant I had a useful range of skills to move into something a little more senior. Which was when I went to the Worcester Swan Theatre which at that point was a small regional producing theatre, so it was a really good theatre for people to learn how to do certain jobs. Not just for people in my job, for a lot of staff there it was their first job at that level, it was a really good sort of training ground.

It's being responsible for everything in the theatre that isn't the work onstage. Although there is a responsibility for the work onstage, it's not a responsibility for creating it, but for making sure that the organisation around the work onstage works, and that includes within it things as various as making sure that you have a good relationship with your funders, so that they fund you and they get the information that they want, to making sure that you have staff in place who can clean the toilets. It's structure, it's organisation, but it's also doing it in a way that has a sympathy with and is integrated into what happens onstage because, particularly in larger theatres, I think there's a real danger that the two things sort of exist separately and I don't think that's what running a theatre is about.

The best aspect of my job is that moment when you are standing at the back of an auditorium and you're watching a production that you know that everybody in the building has contributed to, and you realise that it's working and it's brilliant and also that your audience is totally getting it and that they're all buying tickets to come and see it. So it's getting to the point where there's an end product that works and realising that everybody in some way has had an involvement in it.

The worst bit, I think, is actually dealing with complicated and unhappy staff issues. Because ... 'theatre is all about people' sounds trite, but people are an important part of it. When bits of that don't work the fallout can be really nasty, and it's usually my job to try and sort that out, and that's the bit that I hate most.

Gary Hall

Originally I was a catering person. I did my chef's qualification and wanted to be a chef and that's where I started. When I was at college, I was an usher to pay the bills and in that way I got interested in theatre as well as catering. That was at the Cheltenham Everyman Theatre, so I was working there as an usher then became a chef there at the end of my training. Ninety-five per cent of my catering experience has been within theatre environments – about three or four different venues – and so I progressed to catering manager and running a company at Worcester Swan, which was a thousand-seat theatre, and included the town hall, so we did lots of bigger events. And then I moved to Bristol Old Vic as catering manager and then moved on to looking after everything as theatre manager.

I'd always had an interest in theatre and arts and going to see shows. A treat was a trip to the theatre. We did the annual Christmas thing, and we did school trips. Going to see some strange shows usually when it was a school trip.

Theatre manager? The line I use is that if it's not to do with the production on the stage then, nine out of ten times, I will have a hand in something to do with it. That's everything front of house from the catering to the ushers, to the bookshop, to a little bit of box office. Box office is quite strange because they link in with me and they link in with marketing, but I do have a hand in there. Cleaners, stage door, security, health and safety, it's all that stuff, so it's everything. If it's not to do with the production onstage, then most probably it lands on my desk.

Theatre *is* very conducive to having a restaurant inside it because you can either serve three courses and the diner has a table for the evening, or serve the snack variety that we do very well here. With bars, it's making sure that you've got the right product for your market – most people, if they're coming to the theatre, will buy a drink and an ice cream and a programme. That's their spending power for an evening. So, as long as you've got the right product and you're setting the right margins, then bars will look after themselves actually.

We do a lot of conferences and weddings. So you can get married here, you can have your reception, you can have a disco. Event management is certainly a different skill.

Every day is different – it's why I got involved, I think. Because when you work in hotels or conference venues, then it's the same old thing, day to day. But today's audience is different from tomorrow's. Tonight will be a different audience to the matinee, and we work our menus and what we sell to for those specific markets. We've got to be very proactive to meet the needs of those markets. At the moment we've got lots of schools in so we've got to make sure sweets are visual, very much like a supermarket. If you know you've got lots of children in you get your sweets and ice creams where they can see them and then they'll buy them!

Jane Totney

I'm the assistant to directors, so I work for the executive and artistic directors. The executive director controls the overall running of the theatre budgeting, relationships with the board of directors and basically all the policies and everything that goes into running of the theatre that isn't a production-based job. So a lot of my work for her is administratively based – letters, minutes for meetings, contracts for actors and creative-team members and writers and directors, etc. And then I work also for the artistic director and most of my work for him is around scheduling meetings, liaising with creative-team members, liaising with casting directors and generally all that's related to creative administration. So our office sees the initial stages of a production before anybody else does, in a programming sense as well.

Initially, I come in and check emails. I have to open the post and distribute it to whichever department it goes to. I took a lot of calls yesterday about casting-related things, mostly about a production we're doing next year. I had lots of agents on the phone wanting to know who was casting and whether we'd got anywhere with the casting, etc. I spoke to the writer for our next production who lives in Washington and is coming over, so I'm trying to arrange all his travel and hotels and transport while he's here, as well as mobile phones, so I spent some of the day doing that. I worked on some contracts for the studio productions which are happening next year. We try and get those out really early so if there are any problems for the companies they can get back to us nice and early and we can get things sorted out.

I'd say the best part of my job is speaking to creative teams and making sure they've got everything they need before they get here and generally sort of liaising with them. The worst part of my job – minutes for meetings and filing, although I also have an admin assistant now who has got the unlucky task of doing those bits. So I've grown past filing hopefully!

It's probably a good way in if you are interested in arts management. It's a good place to start because you get to know about every department because you work with every department in the theatre. I also do the personnel side, so I've learnt about HR issues and employment law while I've been in this post.

I think if you secretly want to be an actor or a director then you shouldn't do this job, because you'll never fulfil your desires by being in an administrative job, and maybe you wouldn't do the job to the fullest potential because you're wanting to be somewhere else. Some people think it's a short cut to the stage, and it isn't.

But it's a good way of getting to know how a theatre runs. I didn't have a clue when I was a stage manager – I never met the theatre managers or the administrative directors of the theatres I worked in because they were always very far away in offices.

I think you've got to be outgoing and I think you've got to have a lot of logic. You've got to be a very reactive person because you think you're having a peaceful night and then it suddenly turns chaotic because there's a problem. I don't think there's any wrong or right way of how to get in here. There's the way of going to college because now a lot of colleges are doing theatre-management courses which didn't exist when I was training. I went through the catering line, that's another line. Just getting involved, getting a part-time job, getting a box-office job or a senior ushering job, and then there's always that next step up. I think if you've got the enthusiasm and you're interested in theatre there's always a way to get certainly on to the lower ranks. The further you get up, the harder it is, people are very set when they get to my level, I think.

Most of my days start at ten in the morning. We open up the stage door at eight-thirty, the front doors from ten. Depending on the day, a proportion of it will be spent dealing with front-of-house issues. I then have my financial part of my day, which I always need, to sit down for a couple of hours and look at budgets, targets, re-forecasting how we're doing – the exciting stuff which comes down to me! Then I have to deal with issues – at the moment two staff are at war with each other so I'll spend an hour dealing with that. Then it's really having meetings with directors. We're planning a new menu so I'm getting involved – my house manager and the chef have designed it and we'll have a meeting about that. So every day I have little parts of the day that are very static but I have to be very reactive. Somebody could ring up and want a conference for a thousand people so I have to spend the morning dealing with that, or somebody might walk off the street and want to look around the theatre and I'll have to deal with that, so I think it's being very flexible.

Glossary

Amphitheatre Stepped banks of seating surrounding an arena. Also used to describe one of the tiers of a multilevel auditorium.

Arena A term used to describe a type of open stage. As it derives from the sand-strewn combat area in a Roman amphitheatre, it should be a term for a 360-degree encirclement, but it has been used to describe thrust stages.

Assistant director Assists the director. In many ways the job varies according to the director and the assistant, but it may involve taking some rehearsals, arranging rehearsal calls, making the coffee . . .

Assistant stage manager (ASM) Generally deals with props and will do certain cues during the show. ASMs tend to do cues that involve more direct contact with the actors because the cast will know them from the rehearsal period.

Auditorium The part of the theatre in which the audience sits. Also known as the house.

Backcloth/backdrop A painted or black cloth hung down behind the acting area, hiding the backstage and marking the back of the acting area.

Backlight Light from behind the actor or a piece of scenery. It is a sculptural light which separates the actor from the background.

Backstage The space directly behind or around a stage, accessible only to cast and crew and not usually visible to the audience. Backstage also includes the staff areas (management offices, rehearsal rooms, dressing rooms and workshops).

Bar An aluminium pipe suspended over the stage on which lanterns are hung.

Barn door An arrangement of four metal rectangular plates, on hinges, placed in front of the lenses of fresnel spotlights to control the shape of the light beam.

Batten A long row of floodlights, wired as three or four circuits.

Beam spread The area of light covered by a light beam. The longer the throw, the larger the beam spread.

Beginners The request for cast and crew to take their positions for the start of the performance.

Blackout A fast shutdown of all lighting to complete darkness.

Blacks Curtains hung both to mask the backstage area and to shape the onstage area. Normally made of wool serge.

Blocking The setting of the actors' positions and moves during rehearsals.

Board Another name for a control desk, for either lighting (most usually) or sound.

Book A copy of the script, kept by the deputy stage manager, which includes all cues and notes. Also known as the 'prompt copy'.

Box office The place where the tickets are sold. Occasionally used colloquially to mean the size of the audience ('What's the box office like tonight?').

Box set A set which consists of three walls, around a proscenium arch stage. The proscenium opening is the fourth wall.

Cable Electrical cord used in circuiting lighting equipment needing electricity.

Call The notification to cast and crew of rehearsal or performance. Also the countdown to curtain provided by stage management, usually half-hour call, fifteen-minute call, five-minute call, and beginners. These calls are not the time to the start of the show – they are five minutes earlier; so the thirty-minute call is given thirty-five minutes before the curtain goes up, and so on.

Call board The bulletin board used by stage managers to post any information important to actors and crew, such as rehearsal schedules and costume fittings.

Cans Headphones.

Cast The list of characters in a play and the actors who play them. Also, as a verb, to allocate parts to members of a company.

Centre stage The middle area of the performance space.

Chief electrician Sometimes abbreviated to chief LX, the head of the department responsible for the maintenance and rigging of the lighting, and the operation of the lighting plot. Also usually responsible for the maintenance and repair of anything electrical in the theatre, from the stage lighting to the light in the gents' toilet.

Choreographer Devises and rehearses the dance routines, following the concept laid down by the director.

Colour wash A wash of coloured light over the stage.

Come down In the theatre, a show does not finish – it comes down, i.e. the curtain 'comes down' to end the show.

Commissions Where an artist is appointed to produce a piece of work for the organisation – for instance, a script or video footage.

Company manager While the stage manager deals with what happens onstage, the company manager's job is to look after everything that happens offstage.

Co-production A collaboration between more than one company, to share the creative, scheduling, financial and promotional management of a production.

Corpse Not a dead body in a thriller! An actor who gets an unintended and uncontrollable fit of laughter onstage is said to 'corpse.'

Creative team A group of people assigned to a production to lead the artistic vision and rehearsal process, typically including the director, set, costume, lighting and sound designers, composer, choreographer and fight director.

Crew The backstage group of people who perform all the technical tasks during the show.

Cross In blocking, to move from one area of the stage to another.

Cross-fade Fading one lantern (or group of lanterns) up while fading another down.

Cue The signal for an action by an actor or a technician during a performance. Actors' cues are mostly verbal, but for technicians they may be given verbally over the intercom by the stage manager or visually by a cue light.

Cue lights Lights used by the deputy stage manager to cue backstage technicians and actors.

Cue sheets The pages used to note the cues given by the deputy stage manager to the different technicians.

Curtain In addition to its normal definition relating to draperies, a term used to indicate the start or end of a performance, such as 'Five minutes to curtain up' (five minutes to the start of the performance).

Curtain call Taking a bow in front of the audience at the end of a show.

Cyclorama Plain, curved, stretched cloth or rigid structure used as a background to a setting, giving an illusion of infinity.

Dark theatre A time when there is no performance at the theatre.

Dead The predetermined level to which a suspended scenic piece is raised or lowered to take up its correct position in the setting.

Decibel A measurement of sound intensity. It is not an absolute measure, but measures differing levels relative to each other. Can also be used to measure electrical power. It is a logarithmic measure, with an increase of three decibels indicating a doubling of intensity.

Deputy stage manager (DSM) The deputy to the stage manager. Usually sits on the book and is therefore responsible for the minute-by-minute running of the show.

Designer Designs all aspects of the production: set, costumes, wigs, make-up, etc., unless there are separate designers for costumes, wigs, etc.

Desk See board.

Dimmer An electrical apparatus used to control the intensity of the lantern to which it is circuited.

Dip On a control board, when one cross-fader is brought up and the other brought down simultaneously, there is a dip in the levels of lighting intensity on stage.

Director In control of all aspects of the production. S/he develops the concept of the production, briefs the various designers, plots the actors' moves, rehearses the actors, etc. etc. etc. Each of these, of course, has their own creative input and wise directors (and the best are very wise!) listen carefully to what they have to say. At the end of the day, however, the director has the final word.

Dock The scene dock is a store for scenery next to the stage. Scenery is unloaded and taken through the 'dock door' into the stage area.

Doubling One actor taking more than one part in a play.

Downlight Light from above, the beam perpendicular to the stage floor.

Downstage Portions of a stage nearest the audience.

Dramaturge A person who works alongside writers to develop their plays for performance. Although not necessarily a writer him/herself, a dramaturge's skill lies in knowing what will and won't work onstage. Performs much the same function as a publisher's editor.

Drapes Any unspecified fabric hanging in folds as part of a scene, especially curtaining fabrics such as woollens, velvets, etc.

Dress Abbreviation for dress rehearsal.

Dresser A member of staff who helps actors to get into costume.

Dressing a set The decoration of the set with items that are principally for aesthetic purposes only.

Dress rehearsal The final onstage rehearsal before the first public preview performance, when all costumes, technical effects, props, etc., are used, often for the first time. As close to an actual performance as it is possible to be without an audience present.

Dry Verb: an actor who forgets his words is said to 'dry'.

Dry ice Frozen carbon dioxide particles which, when dropped into hot water, create an effect similar to fog.

Dry tech A technical rehearsal without actors.

DSL Downstage left: towards the front of the stage on the left-hand side as you look at the audience.

DSR Downstage right.

Effects spot A spotlight which projects a slide, or a still, or moving picture, e.g. of rain or clouds, on to the stage or, more usually, the cyclorama.

Electrician A theatre technician who installs and/or operates the lighting for a production.

Entertainment licence Permission granted by a local authority to present a performance to a public audience, providing a series of conditions are met (for instance, a maximum audience capacity in the auditorium).

Fade Sound and lighting term: to increase (fade up), decrease (fade down) or eliminate (fade out) gradually the brightness of a lantern or the volume of a sound.

Fader Part of a lighting or sound desk: by moving a fader up, the volume of the sound or intensity of the light is increased; moving it down decreases volume or intensity.

Feedback An unwanted sound which is produced by the sound from a loudspeaker feeding into a mike and then back through the loudspeaker, creating a loop. Sometimes – appropriately – known as howlround.

Fire curtain A non-flammable curtain hung directly behind the proscenium that protects the audience from fire or smoke emitting from the stage.

First night Also known as opening night or press night. The first night is the public performance to which press critics are invited, at the end of the preview period.

Fit-up The building of the set onstage.

Flat A section of flat scenery, usually made of wood or muslin on a wooden frame.

Flies The space above a stage in which scenery can be flown out of sight of the audience.

Floodlight A lantern that projects a diffused, unfocused beam of light. Used for general illumination.

Floor cloth A heavy piece of muslin used to cover the stage floor.

Focus To direct and 'lock off' a lantern in its specified stage area.

Follow spot A high-intensity spotlight controlled and directed by an operator.

Footlights A series of floodlights placed on the floor along the front of the stage.

Forestage Portion of the stage floor in front of the curtain line.

Fourth wall An imaginary wall between the actors and the audience.

Fresnel A type of lantern that emits a soft-edged diffused light.

Front cloth Sometimes a painted cloth is brought down near to the house curtain for a scene to be played on the forestage. This front cloth usually masks scene changes behind it.

Front light A light coming from downstage of the subject, generally brought in 45 degrees off full front.

Front of house (FoH) The public areas of the theatre, including foyers, auditoriums, restaurants and bars.

FX Effects: usually sound effects in the theatre but can also refer to pyrotechnics. In film, usually refers to visual (i.e. computer-generated) effects.

Gaffer tape A fabric-based sticky tape (black or silver in colour) which is used to fasten down cables temporarily and for 1,001 other uses in theatre. Its big advantage is that, although it adheres firmly to most surfaces, it can be removed without causing any damage to the surface, unlike, for example, Sellotape. Invaluable.

Gauze Flat curtain of fine-mesh netting or similar fabric, either painted or unpainted, which when lit solely from the front appears to be opaque, but when lit from behind becomes transparent. It is used for transformation scenes or other illusions.

G clamp Used for fastening lanterns to a bar. A G-shaped piece of metal with a screw through the bar of the G which clamps to the lighting bar.

Gel Transparent plastic sheet placed in front of a lantern to colour the light beam.

Get-in (and get-out) The process of delivering and taking scenery and props in and out of a theatre.

Gobo A metal cut-out used in spotlights that projects an image onstage. Some modern lights have a number of built-in gobos.

Grand master A fader which masters all the output of a lighting mixer. It controls all preset masters and sub-masters.

Grave trap An oblong trap, usually downstage centre.

Green room A backstage room used by actors and crew as a waiting and meeting area.

Grid The main structure above the stage which supports the flying bars; usually made from steel or, in older theatres, wood.

Ground plan Plan of a stage on which is marked the position of the scenery in a set, including borders, hanging pieces and sometimes lighting equipment.

Half Half an hour before the first actors are due onstage (i.e. thirty-five minutes before the show begins). All actors must be in their dressing rooms by the half. Traditionally, the audience is allowed into the auditorium at that point.

Hand props Properties that are handled by actors during the performance.

House lights Lights used to illuminate the area where the audience sits.

House manager In charge of everything which happens front of house: box office, ushers, bars, cash, etc.

House tabs The curtains across the front of the stage.

Ingénue Old-fashioned term for the female juvenile lead.

Iron The safety curtain.

Juve Abbreviation for juvenile lead: the young male or female main part.

Kilowatt/kW (= 1,000 watts): the power (and therefore brightness) of a lamp. Also used for the power of an electric motor or heating element.

Lamp The part of the lantern that emits the light – in normal use, a bulb. Also called a bubble.

Lamp round The daily check of all lanterns and other lights in a theatre to make sure that lamps do not need replacing.

Lantern A stage light.

Left Stage left, or the left-hand side as you face the audience. Also called the prompt side.

Lighting board The console that controls all the lanterns. Also called the dimmer board and switchboard.

Lighting designer Designs, focuses and plots the lighting for a production. Responsible to the director, not the stage manager. Works in close cooperation with the set designer.

Lighting plan A drawn-up plan that designates the placement of lighting equipment relative to the set. Plan includes gel, circuit and patch number for each lantern.

LX Electrics. The title is given to the lighting department, and the chief electrician is known as the chief LX.

Mask To hide any equipment or offstage area through the use of curtains, flats, etc.

Microphone Usually shortened to mike. An instrument which collects live sound and converts it to electrical impulses which are then put into a mixer/amplifier.

Mirrorball A rotating sphere covered with small plane mirrors. When a spotlight is focused at the ball multiple moving spots of light sweep across surrounding surfaces.

Mixer/mixing desk A device for mixing together and modifying sounds from a variety of sources – microphones, tapes, CDs, musical instruments, etc. – before feeding them into one or more amplifiers.

Monitor A special kind of speaker which is used to monitor the sound (either onstage or in the lighting/sound box) and which is not relayed to the audience.

Mr Sands Theatrical code to warn theatre employees of a fire without frightening the audience. 'Mr Sands is in the foyer' means that a fire has broken out in the foyer.

Musical director (MD) In charge of the music in the production, under the overall control of the director. Rehearses the singers and musicians, conducts the orchestra or band, and usually arranges the music too.

Notes The director's comments at the end of each rehearsal or performance.

Offstage Any position on the stage floor out of sight of the audience.

Onstage Any position on the stage within the acting area.

On the book When either the deputy stage manager or an assistant is following the script in order to help actors when they stumble over lines.

Pace The tempo of the performance.

Paint bridge A platform or wide cradle the width of the paint frame which can be hauled up and down, usually mechanically, so that all parts of a cloth can be reached.

Paint frame The frame to which backcloths, flats, etc., are fixed for painting in a vertical position.

Paper the house To give away free tickets to a performance in order to fill the house.

Parcan A type of lantern which projects a near parallel beam of light, much used by rock bands. The lamp is a sealed-beam unit (like car headlights) fitted inside the 'can'. Sometimes known as parblazers or beamlights.

Pass door A door connecting the front of house with the backstage area.

Patch To connect a circuit to a dimmer.

Patch panel The board on which lighting circuits are connected to dimmers.

Pebble convex A type of spotlight, with a harder-edged beam than a fresnel but softer than a profile. They have a convex lens with a pebbled rear surface. Sometimes known as prism convex.

Per diems Very important to actors: the daily expenses paid on tour.

Photo call The acting company run a selection of scenes from a new production, in costume, for the benefit of photographers whose pictures will illustrate press reviews.

Pit The area below the front of the stage. May be used to house the orchestra. Also called the orchestra pit.

Plot The brightness settings of each lantern and the LX cues. Also used to describe the process of setting the cues.

Preset The setting onstage that the audience sees before the play begins; refers to light, set and props.

Previews The first public performances of a production, leading to first night. Changes to script, performances and all other aspects of the show can be (and often are) made during previews.

Producer The person who chooses a play, assembles a creative team, agrees budgets and contracts, and oversees all aspects of a production and its promotion from inception to completion.

Profile spot A type of spotlight (qv), with an optical system rather like a projector which produces a narrow, hard-edged beam of light.

Programme An illustrated publication accompanying a production, which provides the audience with background information about the cast and creative team, and essays relating to the play.

Prompt To give an actor a line when he or she either asks or is stumbling.

Prompt copy/script The notebook kept by the deputy/stage manager that contains all paperwork necessary to the production of the play, including a script with blocking and cues. Also called the book.

Prompt corner The area from which the deputy stage manager runs the show. Usually found just to the right or left of the proscenium backstage. Otherwise, the DSM might sit in the lighting or sound booth to call the show.

Props Objects or items of furniture used in a performance (but not including scenery). Categorised into 'hand props' and 'set props' (or 'set dressing').

Prop table The table backstage on which props are laid out, usually in a mapped-out order.

Proscenium arch The traditional picture-frame type of stage, usually with a curtain. Often abbreviated to 'pros' arch.

Pyrotechnics Used in performance to create visual and sound effects of explosions, fire, gunshots, etc. Pyrotechnics can be hazardous and are controlled by licensing and safety regulations.

Quick change A fast costume change.

Radio mike Also known as a wireless mike. A mike incorporating a small radio transmitter which sends its signal to a receiver which is attached to a mixer. This does away with the need for trailing cables. Note that only certain radio frequencies can be used without a licence.

Rake Some stage floors are higher at the back than at the front, to give the audience a better view. These stages are said to be 'raked', and the 'rake' is the angle of slope from back to front. In most modern theatres it is the audience seating that is raked, not the stage.

Ramp Inclined rostrum, normally sloping up from the stage floor.

Read-through Usually the first rehearsal at which the company reads through the script.

Repertoire A group of plays presented in a season. The combination of plays will be carefully considered to ensure compatibility and variety.

Repertory A cyclical system of scheduling performances when several plays (a repertoire) are staged over the course of a season. A typical repertory pattern may see one play from the repertoire presented for a week, then swapped with another play to be presented on the same stage. The repertory system allows theatres to stage more productions in a year and to extend the length of time they are playing. A number of actors are employed to become company members and may be cast in several plays in the repertoire.

Revolve A stage or, more usually, part of a stage (usually circular) which can revolve through 360 degrees. Can be used for a quick scene change or for creating various effects.

Rig To set the lanterns in position or to set up scenery onstage. Rigging is a collective term for the suspension of equipment. De-rigging is taking it down again.

Right Stage right, or the right-hand side as you face the audience. Also called the prompt side.

Rostrum A platform placed on the stage floor to create changes of level where required.

Run The total number of performances for a production.

Run-through A rehearsal of the show which is performed from beginning to end without stopping.

Safety chain A metal chain or wire used as a backup to prevent a lantern falling from the lighting rig if the clamp fails.

Safety curtain A screen or shutter of fireproofed material, usually with a metal frame, mounted just behind the proscenium opening and fitted with a mechanism for raising it clear of the top of the proscenium arch and with a quick-release device to allow it to descend in the event of fire on the stage. In many theatres it is also used during the interval.

Sandbag Bag of canvas with strap and ring, filled with sand and used for weighting purposes.

Scene changes The transformation of the stage set between scenes or acts in a play, to give the effect of a change in location or time.

Set The scenery for a particular show or individual scene.

Set dressing Props that are used to decorate the set and are usually not handled by actors.

Sidelight Light from the side of an actor facing the audience. Side lighting is often used in dance, as it emphasises the entire body and movement.

Sightlines The area of the stage which can be seen by those seated in the auditorium. In some theatres, a member of the audience sitting at the end of certain rows, might only see two-thirds of the stage.

Smoke machine A machine which produces the effect of a haze of smoke or light in the air by heating up a harmless smoke fluid.

Snap cue A cue executed in an instant.

Special A lantern used for one specific object or effect.

Spill Extraneous light from a lantern that can be cut off with a shutter.

Spotlight A type of lantern whose beam is focused through a lens or series of lenses to make it more controllable. Often abbreviated to 'spot'.

Staff directors Assigned by a theatre to a specific production, staff directors attend rehearsals and assist the director and creative team. Once a play has opened to the public, they direct the understudy rehearsals and oversee the run of performances, giving directorial notes to the company where required.

Stage brace Adjustable device comprising two lengths of wood sliding one along the other and held fast by clamps; used to prop scenery from behind.

Stage cloth Large piece of canvas, used to cover the stage floor, often painted to represent paving etc.

Stage directions Instructions indicating the movement or blocking of the performers, and other descriptions of the physical setting or atmosphere of the play.

Stage door The entrance into the theatre for all personnel involved in the show. It is usually small and unobtrusive and well away from the door(s) through which the audience enter. It is presided over by the stage doorman or doorkeeper.

Stage left Actor's left.

Stage manager (SM) In charge of everything that happens backstage: all technical backstage personnel, including heads of departments, report to him. Once the show starts its run, the stage manager takes control.

Stage right Actor's right.

State Refers to the lanterns and their dimmer and colour settings, used in a particular cue. During the plotting of the lighting, the operator may be told to 'go back to a state of 2', which means to set the dimmers as they were in cue 2.

Strike Remove set, scenery, props, costumes or lights from the acting area after they have been used, usually at the end of an act, performance or run.

Strobe A lantern which emits a regular, controllable series of high-power flashes rather than continuous light. Note: strobes can induce fits in epileptics and so warnings about their use should always be given before the show starts.

Surround Set of legs (ordinary pleated curtains) hung from a curved or angled bar to form the sides and background to an acting area.

Swatch A small piece of fabric or paint used to demonstrate the colour and/or texture of the material being used.

Tabs The curtains which close across the proscenium arch are called 'house tabs'.

Tallescope Scaffolding on wheels for moving around the stage to rig and focus lanterns.

Techies Theatre slang for the technical crew

Technical rehearsal The rehearsal or series of rehearsals in which the technical elements of the show – scenery, lighting, sound, video, props – are integrated with the work of the actors. Cues and scene changes are rehearsed and perfected to ensure that everything proceeds seamlessly onstage, and cast and crew members know where they need to be at all times during a performance. Also called the tech.

Theatre-in-the-round A way of staging a play in which the audience sits on all sides of the stage.

Thrust stage A type of theatre in which the audience is seated on three sides of the stage.

Touring The process of taking a play from the repertoire, or a brand-new production, to a number of arts venues across the country or internationally.

Trap A trapdoor set in the stage floor.

Traps Removable areas of the stage floor that allow access to the area underneath the stage. Special-purpose traps are grave traps, dip traps and star traps.

Understudy An actor employed to be a replacement in case of indisposition of an actor appearing in a play. The understudies will learn and rehearse their appointed role and be available to step in if required.

Unions Equity, BECTU, Musicians' Union – independent bodies who mediate between staff and employers to ensure that employment conditions and standards are met and maintained. Equity represents actors and stage managers; BECTU is a union for technical and production staff; and the Musicians' Union represents musicians and composers.

Unsolicited scripts Scripts that are submitted by playwrights for consideration, without having been commissioned or specifically requested. The National Theatre receives 1,500 unsolicited scripts every year.

Upstage The portions of the stage furthest from the audience. To move upstage means to move away from the audience. As a verb: when one actor deliberately draws the attention of the audience away from another actor to him/herself.

Ushers Oversee the smooth traffic of visitors from the foyers into the auditorium. Ushers are also on hand to direct and guide audience members in case of emergencies.

USL Upstage left.

USR Upstage right.

Wardrobe supervisor Responsible for the making (under the direction of the designer), repair and washing of all costumes.

Wash light Light used to give a general illumination of the stage; quite often a specific colour is used in a wash.

Wings Offstage spaces to the left and right of the acting area, where actors stand before making their entrance, and where props are kept, ready to be brought on to the stage.

Work lights Lights used for general illumination of the stage when not in performance.